QUILTS DU [illegible]R

MAKE IT YOUR OWN WITH À LA CARTE BLOCKS & SETTINGS

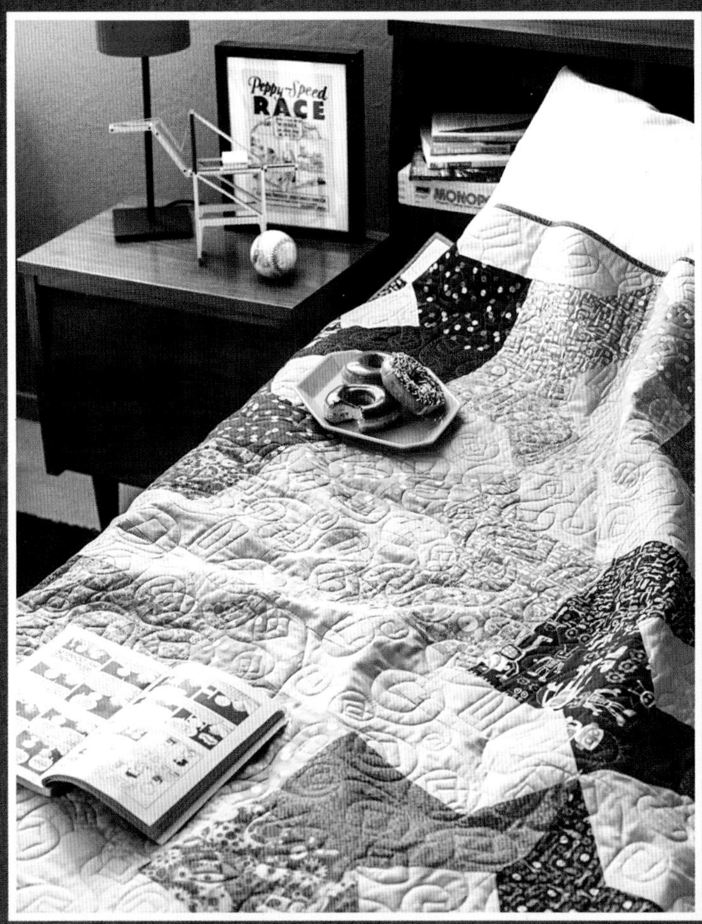

MARNY BUCK *and* JILL GUFFY

stashBOOKS®
an imprint of C&T Publishing

Publisher: Amy Marson

Creative Director: Gailen Runge

Art Director/Cover Designer: Kristy Zacharias

Editor: Karla Menaugh

Technical Editors: Debbie Rodgers and Gailen Runge

Book Designer: Casey Dukes

Production Coordinator: Jenny Davis

Production Editor: Katie Van Amburg

Illustrator: Jessica Jenkins

Photo Assistant: Mary Peyton Peppo

Style photography by Nissa Brehmer and instructional photography by Diane Pedersen, unless otherwise noted

Published by Stash Books, an imprint of C&T Publishing, Inc., P.O. Box 1456, Lafayette, CA 94549

Library of Congress Cataloging-in-Publication Data
Buck, Marny, 1953-
Quilts du jour : make it your own with à la carte blocks & settings / Marny Buck and Jill Guffy.
pages cm
Includes index.
ISBN 978-1-61745-071-6 (soft cover)
1. Patchwork quilts. 2. Patchwork--Patterns. 3. Square in art. 4. Rectangles in art.
I. Guffy, Jill, 1950- II. Title.
TT835.B759 2015
746.46--dc23
2015003029

Printed in China
10 9 8 7 6 5 4 3 2 1

DEDICATION

Simply, we dedicate this to our families, our friends, and those who have challenged and inspired us. It wouldn't have happened or have been as much fun without you (or without one another)!

ACKNOWLEDGMENTS

We thank April West, our longarm quilter, for adjusting to our timeline, collaborating on quilting decisions, and her continued friendship and support.

We are grateful for the generosity of the fabric manufacturers and their designers. Our thanks go to Benartex, Dear Stella Design, P&B Textiles, Robert Kaufman Fabrics, and Studio E Fabrics.

We appreciate the talents and advice of our editors, designers, photographers, and illustrators at C&T. They helped us bring our book from the kitchen to the table!

TABLE OF CONTENTS

SELECT YOUR OWN GREAT QUILT FROM FOUR MENUS 4
TECHNIQUES 6

Appetizer Menu

SIX ENTICING BLOCKS 11

Crudités Block 12
Salsa Block 16
Crispy Wonton Block 22
Celery Sticks Block 26
It's a Wrap Block 32
Sushi Block 38

Tasting Menu

QUILT PROJECTS TO SATISFY CRAVINGS 43

Antipasto Platter 44
Snack Circuit 48
Bottle Stoppers 52
Dippers 56
Mondrian Morsels 60
Spring Rolls 64

Settings Menu

SIZE AND LAYOUT OPTIONS TO MAKE IT YOUR OWN 69

Grid Setting 70
Repeated Horizontal Setting 72
Diagonal-Line Setting 76
Straight-Line Setting 80
Staggered Setting 84
Radiating Setting 86

Dessert Menu

TASTY ALTERNATIVE QUILT PROJECTS 89

Tempting Turnovers 90
Easy as Pie 96
Éclairs 102
Glycemic Index 106
Petits Fours 112
Sweet Endings 118

SAVORY BACKING SUGGESTIONS 122
ABOUT THE AUTHORS 127
RESOURCES 127

SELECT YOUR OWN GREAT QUILT FROM FOUR MENUS

We relish the unforgettable meals that result from creative menus filled with new flavors and food combinations. *Quilts du Jour* offers inspiring menus to encourage you to create your own memorable quilt from a variety of tempting selections.

APPETIZER MENU: SIX ENTICING BLOCKS

Start exploring here to discover ingredients and directions for six modern blocks finishing either 8″ or 16″ square. The blocks work as modules to be placed in a variety of multisized settings. We show them put together in pillows.

TASTING MENU: QUILT PROJECTS TO SATISFY CRAVINGS

Each block, showcasing solid fabrics, is featured in a quilt illustrating one of six layouts.

SETTINGS MENU: SIZE AND LAYOUT OPTIONS TO MAKE IT YOUR OWN

Six layouts diagrammed in a variety of block- and quilt-size formats, plus background yardage and cutting measurements. You choose the block and get cooking!

DESSERT MENU: TASTY ALTERNATIVE QUILT PROJECTS

Take a peek to find fresh fabric and setting alternatives for each block. No need to worry about the calories!

SAVORY BACKING SUGGESTIONS

Explore the backs of our quilts for design solutions to make your quilt backs more interesting.

Create quilts that suit your taste and style! Sample from the blocks as much or as little as you like. Follow up by placing them in your choice of settings. These are your quilts, and we hope you enjoy the process!

We love designing modern quilts. Our quilts feature design elements and principles seen in midcentury modern architecture. Our designs emphasize asymmetry, negative space, simple shapes, and the use of color and value to provide depth and focus.

Block and setting designs, color schemes, quilting ideas, binding choices, and more are shared throughout *Quilts du Jour*.

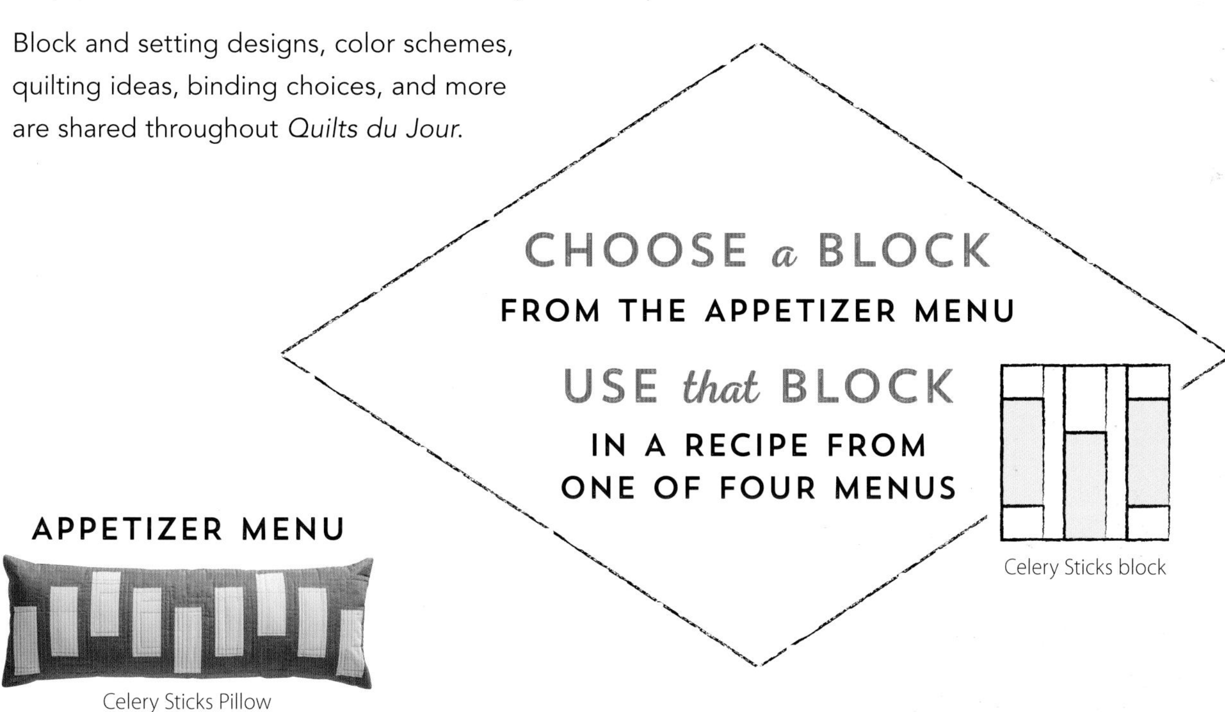
CHOOSE a BLOCK
FROM THE APPETIZER MENU
USE that BLOCK
IN A RECIPE FROM
ONE OF FOUR MENUS
APPETIZER MENU

Celery Sticks block

Celery Sticks Pillow

TASTING MENU

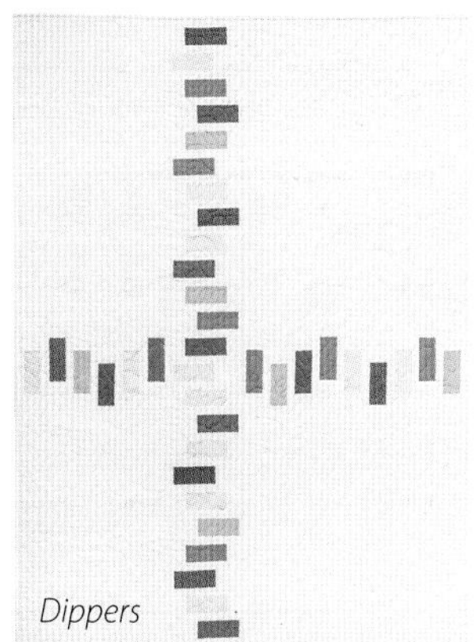

Dippers

SETTINGS MENU

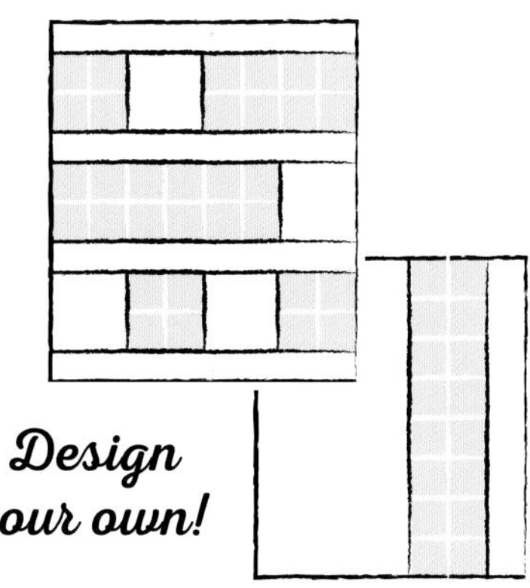
Design
your own!

DESSERT MENU

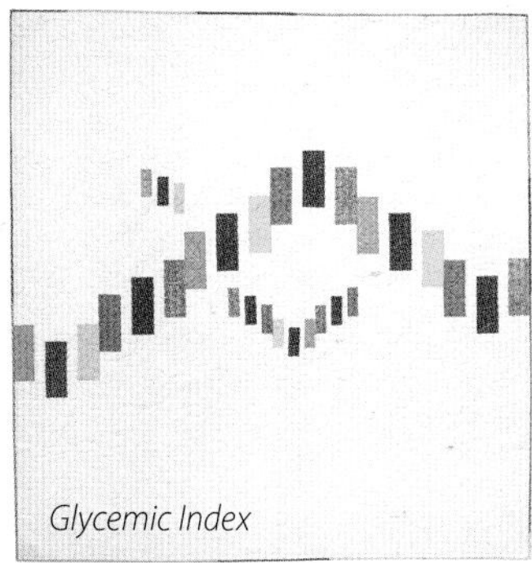

Glycemic Index

TECHNIQUES

This chapter is a brief overview of some of our favorite quilt-making techniques. You can learn more about the basics, such as how to use rotary-cutting equipment, layering and basting a quilt, machine quilting, hand quilting, or how to bind a quilt, by taking a class at your local quilt shop or online. See Resources (page 127) for some book ideas and a link to C&T Publishing's quilting and sewing tips.

ROTARY CUTTING WITH TWO RULERS

We use this technique almost exclusively! The advantage of the two-ruler method is that it allows you to cut strips from a length of folded fabric without moving the fabric. It's also easier to cut large pieces of fabric. The following directions show you how to cut strips or larger pieces. You can adjust the width to cut whatever sizes you need.

CUTTING 2″ STRIPS

1. On the right end of the folded fabric, position a horizontal line of a ruler with the bottom fold of fabric. Cut along the right edge of the ruler to straighten the edges of the folded fabric.

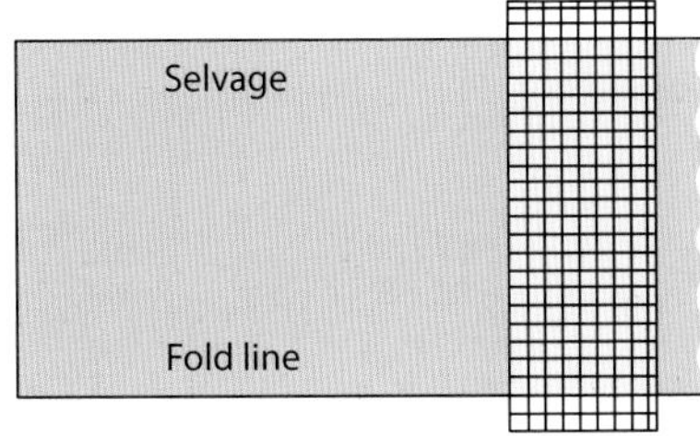

2. Place the first ruler with the 2″ marking aligned along the clean edge of the fabric, making sure the ruler is square with the bottom fold.

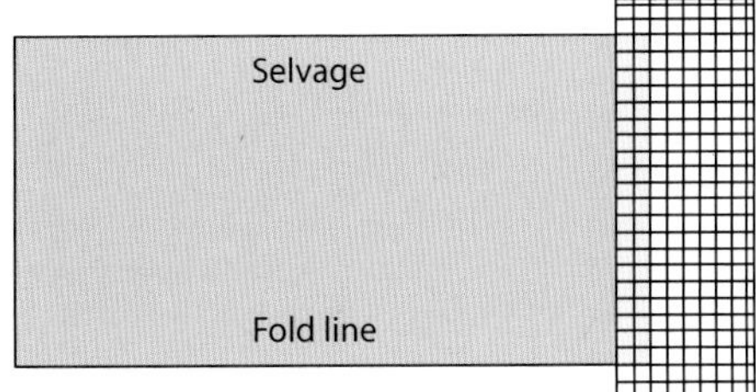

3. Place a second ruler against the left side of the first ruler. Check that both rulers are square with the bottom folded edge of the fabric and that the 2″ vertical line of the first ruler is still aligned with the clean edge.

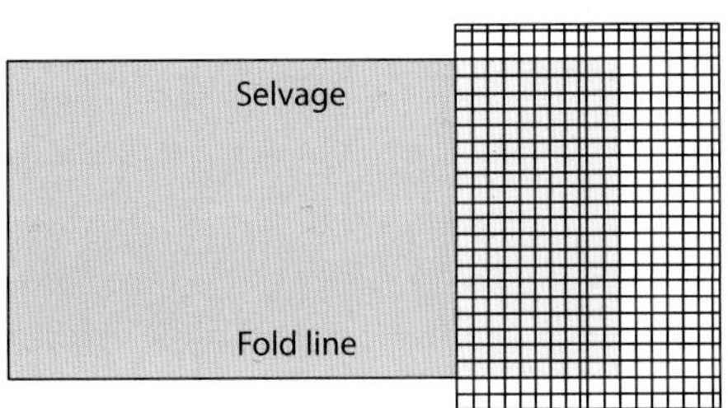

The Best Ruler Sizes

If we could buy only three rulers, we would buy the 8½″ square, the 16½″ square, and the 8½″ × 24½″ rectangle. These three are the workhorses of the sewing room, useful for cutting yardage and squaring up blocks.

4. Take the first ruler away.

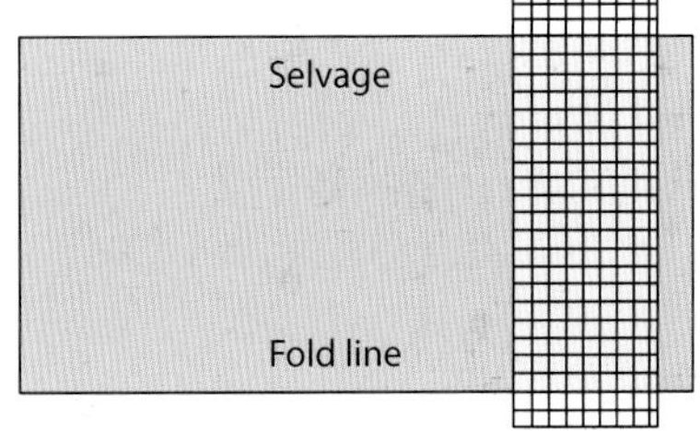

5. Cut along right edge of second ruler to yield a 2″ strip.

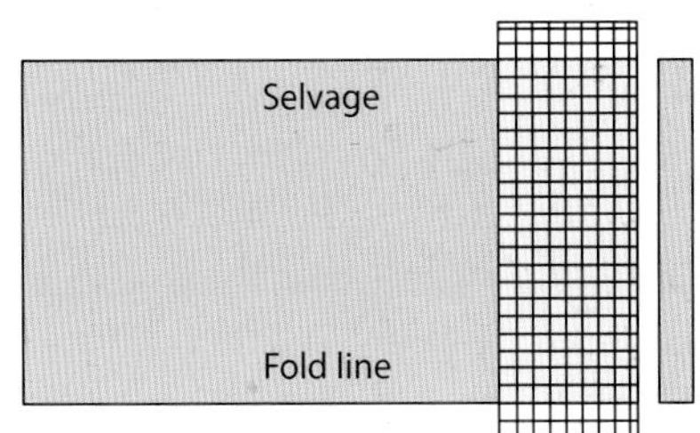

CUTTING LARGE PIECES

1. Straighten the right edge of the fabric in the same manner as in Cutting 2″ Strips, Step 1 (page 7).

2. To measure a 16½″ strip, position a 24½″ ruler parallel to the fold in the fabric with the 16½″ mark along the cut edge. Place a second ruler on the left side of the first ruler. Make sure the horizontal markings on both rulers are square with the folded edge of the fabric.

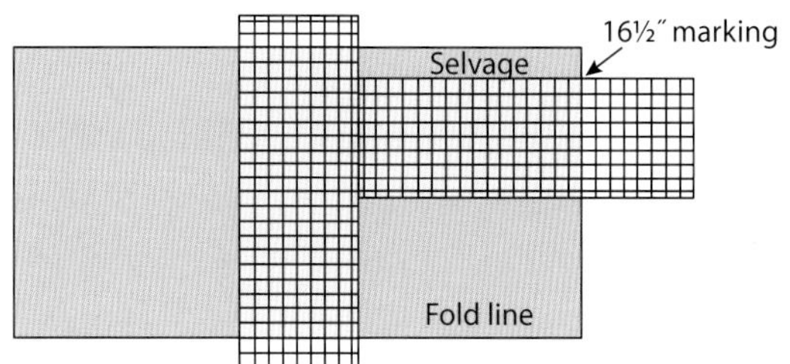

3. Take the first ruler away and cut along the right edge of the second ruler.

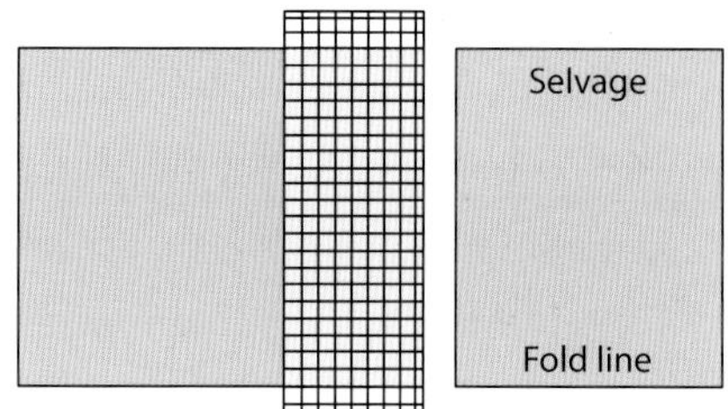

FINISHING YOUR QUILT

Refer to Resources (page 127) for the link to "How to Finish Your Quilt," a downloadable PDF available at ctpub.com, for information on layering, basting, and binding your quilt. Our binding yardages are based on the double-fold straight-grain binding described in the document, except with a 2½″ cut width to create a ⅜″ finished binding.

We love to completely machine stitch the bindings on our quilts, so we share our method here.

How to Finish Your Quilt
PDF AVAILABLE AT CTPUB.COM

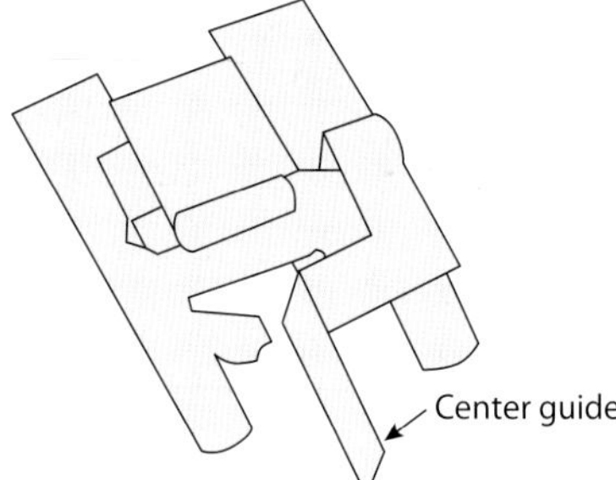

BINDING BY MACHINE

Our bindings are entirely machine sewn. After the usual steps of attaching the binding from the front side of the quilt, pressing, folding the binding to the back of the quilt, and securing it with binding clips, we machine stitch our binding down from the front. Using an edge-joining foot ensures success!

The edge-joining foot has a center guide that can ride along the seamline where the binding is sewn to the project.

You might need to move the needle one or two positions closer to the binding (to the right). Check after stitching a few inches to be sure the stitching is in the right place on the back. Then away you go!

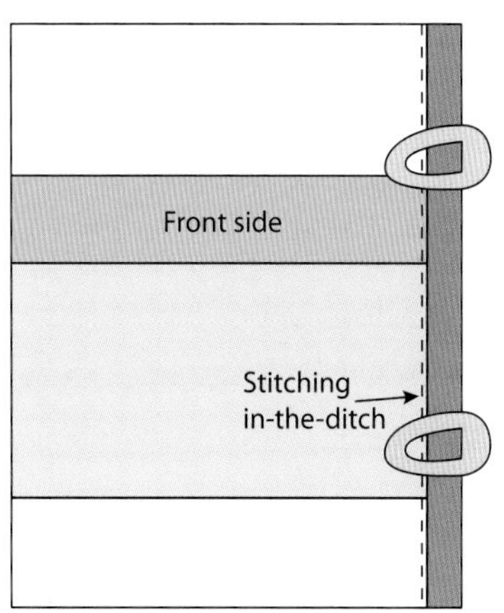

This method results in a nice finish on both the top and the back of the quilt. The more you practice, the better you will get. Figuring out how big a seam allowance to use when attaching the binding might take a bit of experimentation at first. Start with ¼″, but change it depending on the thickness of the batting. A thicker batting will need a narrower seam allowance; a thinner batting will need a wider seam allowance. The key is to have some binding on the back side to catch with your line of stitching from the front side, but not too much.

Detail of *Snack Circuit* (see project photo, page 51) showing binding from front

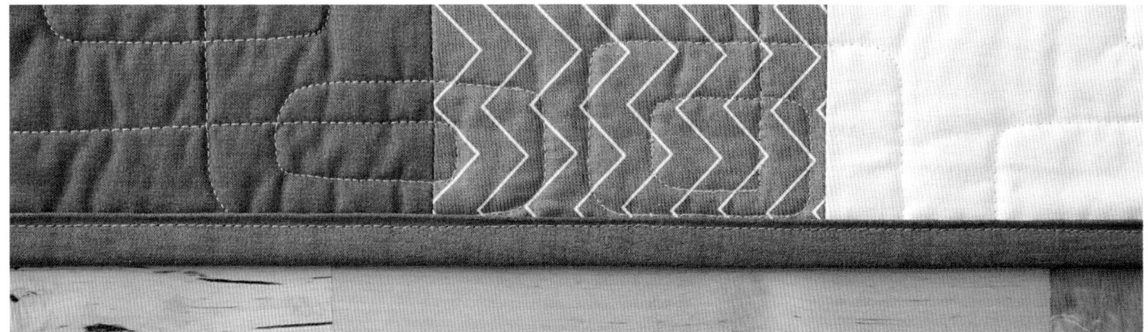

Detail of *Snack Circuit* (see project photo, page 51) showing binding from back

FINISHING YOUR PILLOW

PILLOW WITH OVERLAPPED BACK

If you plan to use a pillow insert, make an overlapped back for ease of adding or removing the insert.

1. You need 2 backing pieces. To determine the width of the backing pieces, divide the width of the pillow top, including the seam allowance, in half; then add 3″. Cut 2 backing pieces this width and the same length as the pillow top. For the 16″ finished square pillows we show in the Appetizer Menu (pages 11–42), cut 2 backing pieces 11¼″ × 16½″.

2. Turn under ¼″ along a 16½″ edge of each backing piece and press. Fold again ¾″ and press. Topstitch ⅛″ from the inner folded edge of each to create a hem.

3. Place a pillow back rectangle facedown on top of the pillow front, with the hemmed edge toward the center and the raw edges of the backing piece lined up with the raw edges of the top, and pin.

4. Place the remaining pillow back rectangle facedown on the other side of the pillow front, raw edges matching. The finished edges of the back rectangles will overlap in the center. Pin. Stitch with a ¼″ seam allowance, backstitching at the beginning and end.

5. Trim the corners at a diagonal and turn the pillow right side out. Insert a 16″ × 16″ pillow form.

PILLOW WITH CLOSED BACK

If your pillow is an unusual size, such as our 28″ × 10″ Celery Sticks pillow (page 26), you probably will fill the pillow with polyfill. To make sure the polyfill stays in place, use a closed pillow back.

1. Cut a back piece exactly the same unfinished size as the pillow top, 28½″ × 10½″ for the Celery Sticks pillow.

2. Place the top and back right sides together and stitch a ¼″ seam around the perimeter, leaving a 3″ opening at the bottom for stuffing. Backstitch at the beginning and the end.

3. Trim the corners at a diagonal and turn the pillow right side out. Insert the polyfill and hand stitch the opening closed.

APPETIZER MENU

SIX ENTICING BLOCKS

Crudités Block	**12**	Celery Sticks Block	**26**
Salsa Block	**16**	It's a Wrap Block	**32**
Crispy Wonton Block	**22**	Sushi Block	**38**

Browse the collection of six modern blocks—tasty appetizers meant to inspire from the very first bite. We have included recipes for each block in either 8˝ or 16˝ sizes.

We used our sample 8˝ blocks to make pillows. The 16˝ sample blocks are perfect for creating table or bed runners. In the Tasting Menu (pages 43–68) and Dessert Menu (pages 89–121), each block reappears in quilts illustrating different settings.

To design your own quilt, choose a block design and refer to the Settings Menu (pages 66–88) to choose a size and a setting. To determine your fabric requirements, divide the number of blocks you need by the number of blocks your chosen recipe yields. Multiply that number by the block recipe's yardage requirements. For example, if you need twenty blocks and the block recipe makes four blocks, divide twenty by four to get five. Multiply the yardage requirements from the block recipe by five to see how much fabric you will need. You can find additional background yardage and cutting instructions in the Settings Menu.

Great appetizers can set the stage for special meals. Find your inspiration and get cooking!

Combine four 8˝ Salsa blocks to make one spicy pillow!

CRUDITÉS BLOCK

CRUDITÉS PILLOW, 16″ × 16″
MADE BY MARNY BUCK, 2014

The Crudités pillow is made from 8″ blocks, 1 each of A, B, C, and D.

Crudités is made up of four components: two half-square triangle units, a bar of color set in background, and a plain background square. The components can be combined in countless ways. The interplay among seemingly random simple shapes creates energy and secondary shapes. The plain quadrant in each block builds a large proportion of negative space into the overall design, reflecting our modern aesthetic.

Antipasto Platter (page 44) on the Tasting Menu uses this dynamic 8″ block in a regular grid setting. The 16″ block is featured in a radiating setting in *Tempting Turnovers* (page 90) on the Dessert Menu.

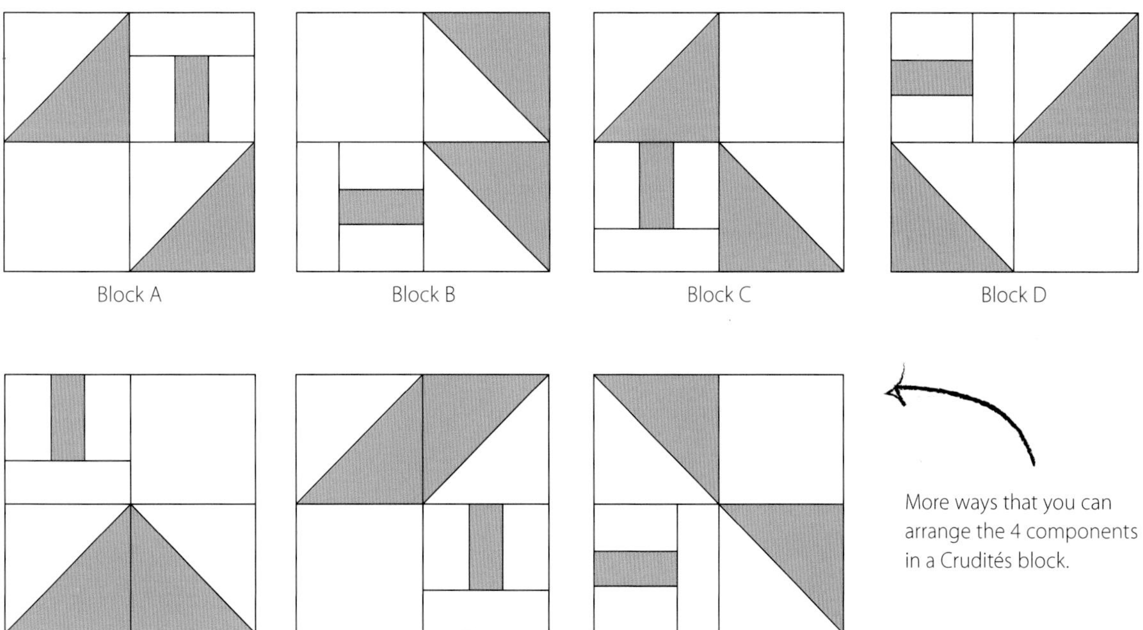

More ways that you can arrange the 4 components in a Crudités block.

CRUDITÉS BLOCK RECIPE

Finished blocks: 8″ × 8″ (as shown in pillow) or 16″ × 16″

Ingredients

- **Color:** ¼ yard (½ yard)
- **Background:** ⅓ yard (1 yard)

These yardages will make 4 blocks and are based on 42″ of usable width from nondirectional fabrics. These are minimum yardage requirements, without much extra for cutting errors. You might choose to buy extra.

Prep the Ingredients

Cut all fabrics by the width of fabric. Remove selvages before cutting.

CUTTING FOR 8″ BLOCKS

FROM THE COLOR:

- Cut 1 strip 5″ × width of fabric.
  Subcut 4 squares 5″ × 5″.
  Subcut 1 strip 1½″ × 21″.

FROM THE BACKGROUND:

- Cut 1 strip 5″ × width of fabric.
  Subcut 4 squares 5″ × 5″.
  Subcut 4 squares 4½″ × 4½″.
- Cut 1 strip 2″ × width of fabric.
  Subcut 2 rectangles 2″ × 21″.
- Cut 1 strip 1¾″ × width of fabric.
  Subcut 4 rectangles 1¾″ × 4½″.

CUTTING FOR 16″ BLOCKS

FROM THE COLOR:

- Cut 1 strip 9¼″ × width of fabric.
  Subcut 4 squares 9¼″ × 9¼″.
- Cut 1 strip 2½″ × width of fabric.

FROM THE BACKGROUND:

- Cut 1 strip 9¼″ × width of fabric.
  Subcut 4 squares 9¼″ × 9¼″.
- Cut 1 strip 8½″ × width of fabric.
  Subcut 4 squares 8½″ × 8½″.
- Cut 2 strips 3½″ × width of fabric.
- Cut 1 strip 3″ × width of fabric.
  Subcut 4 rectangles 3″ × 8½″.

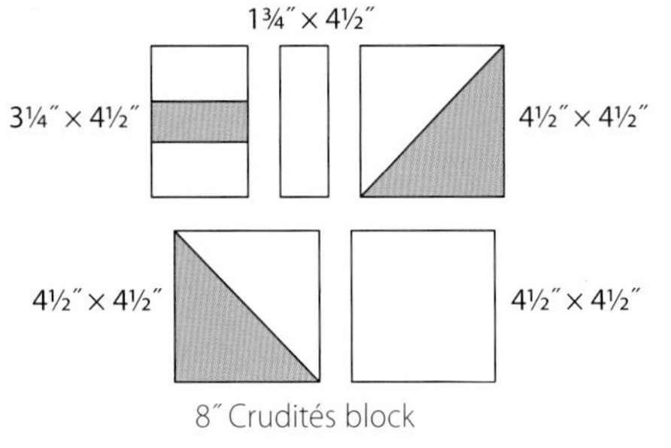

8″ Crudités block

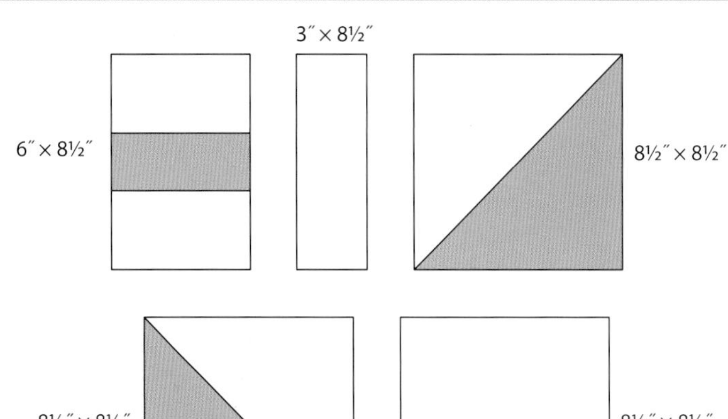

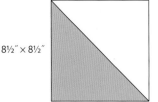

16″ Crudités block

MAKE THE BLOCK

The first number in parentheses is for 8″ blocks; the second number is for 16″ blocks. The construction steps are the same for both sizes. Use ¼″ seams. Gently press all seams as you work, taking special care with any bias seams. For a flat, finished look, press all seams open.

1. Mark diagonally, corner to corner, on the wrong side of the (5″, 9¼″) background squares.

2. Stack each background square right sides together with a (5″, 9¼″) color square. Stitch ¼″ away from each side of the drawn line.

3. Cut on the drawn line. Press the seam open.

4. Repeat Step 3 for the remaining sets. Trim the resulting 8 half-square triangles to (4½″, 8½″) square. Set aside.

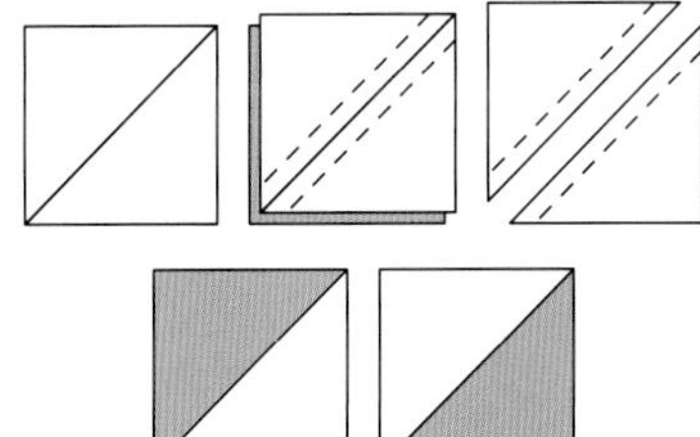

5. Sew a (2″ × 21″, 3½″ × width of fabric) background strip to each side of the (1½″ × 21″, 2½″ × width of fabric) color strip.

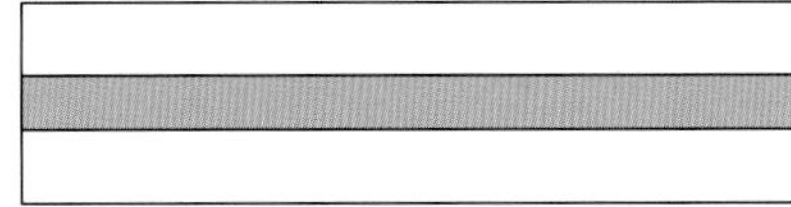

6. Cut 4 segments at (3¼″, 6″) intervals.

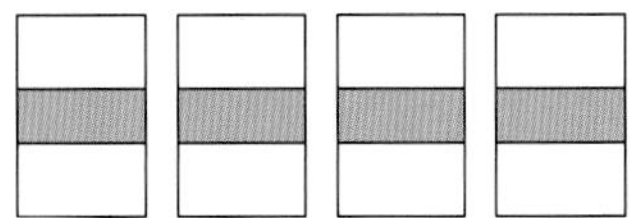

7. Sew a (1¾″ × 4½″, 3″ × 8½″) background rectangle to each Step 6 unit.

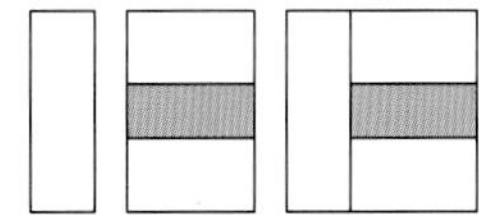

8. Sew 2 Step 4 units, a Step 7 unit, and a (4½″, 8½″) plain background square together to make 1 each A, B, C, and D block (or any arrangement you choose).

ASSEMBLE THE PILLOW

Piece 4 blocks together in a 2 × 2 configuration.

Refer to Pillow with Overlapped Back (page 10) for instructions on finishing your pillow.

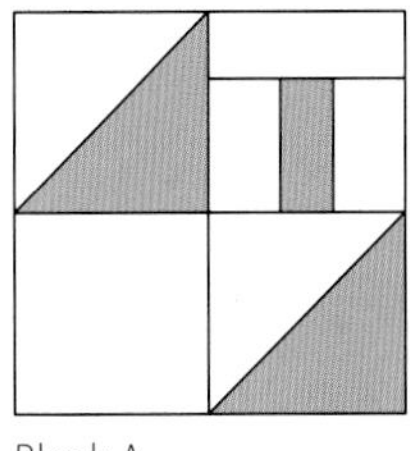

Block A

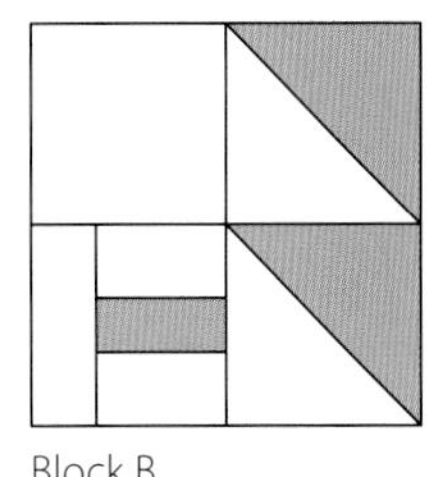

Block B

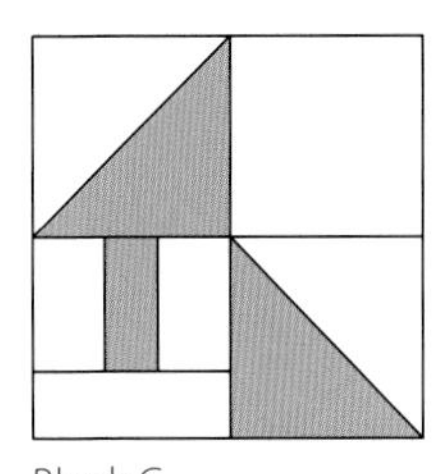

Block C

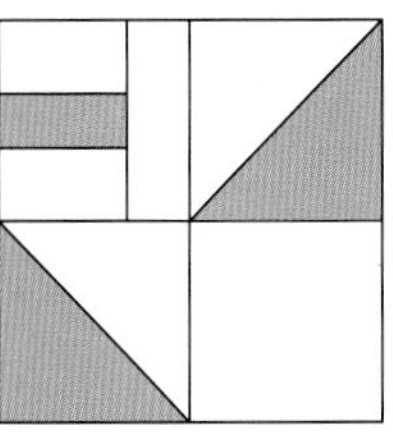

Block D

SALSA BLOCK

SALSA PILLOW, 16″ × 16″
MADE BY JILL GUFFY, 2014

The Salsa pillow is made from 8″ blocks, 1 each A, B, C, and D.

Salsa is a series of four blocks. Two blocks, slightly different in their arrangement, along with their mirror images, make this pillow. The graphic design is created with carefully chosen values proportionally balanced with negative space. Using a range of five values, from dark to light, clarifies the shapes and edges within the block. In this pillow, the white negative space takes on a shape rather than acting as a background. The twists and turns of the arrangements offer endless combinations.

Snack Circuit (page 48) on the Tasting Menu displays the 8″ blocks in a horizontal setting. *Easy as Pie* (page 96) on the Dessert Menu illustrates the 16″ block in a simple vertical setting.

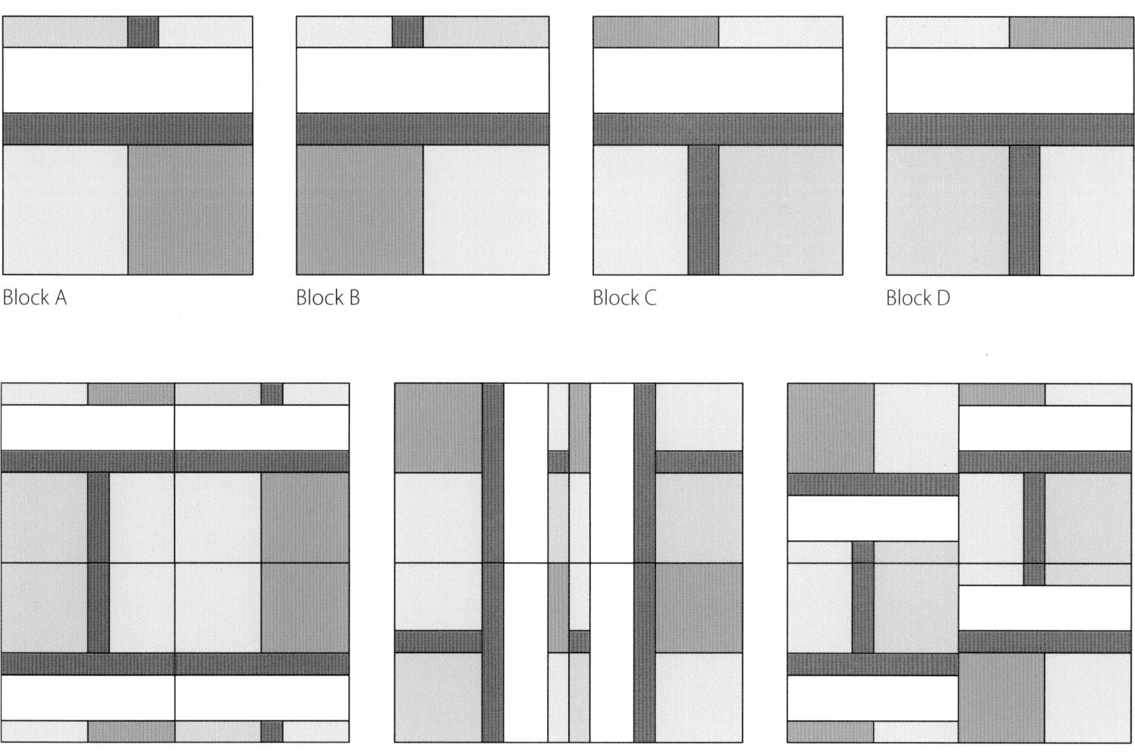

Additional setting options for 4 Salsa blocks

SALSA BLOCK RECIPE

Finished blocks: 8″ × 8″ (as shown in pillow) or 16″ × 16″

Ingredients

Use 5 distinct values to read high contrast. We used 3 related greens with good contrast between the values, a red accent, and white.

- **Fabric 1 (light green):** ⅙ yard (½ yard)
- **Fabric 2 (dark green):** ⅙ yard (⅓ yard)
- **Fabric 3 (medium green):** ⅙ yard (⅓ yard)
- **Fabric 4 (white):** ⅛ yard (⅓ yard)
- **Accent (red):** ⅛ yard (¼ yard)

These yardages will make 4 blocks and are based on 42″ of usable width from nondirectional fabrics. These are minimum yardage requirements. You might choose to buy extra.

Prep the Ingredients

Cut all fabrics by the width of fabric. Remove selvages before cutting.

CUTTING FOR 8″ BLOCKS

FROM FABRIC 1:

- Cut 1 strip 4½″ × width of fabric.

  Subcut 1 rectangle 4½″ × 21″

  Subcut 1 rectangle 3½″ × 21″.

FROM FABRIC 2:

- Cut 1 strip 4½″ × width of fabric.

  Subcut 1 rectangle 4½″ × 21″.

FROM FABRIC 3:

- Cut 1 strip 4½″ × width of fabric.

  Subcut 1 rectangle 4½″ × 21″.

FROM FABRIC 4:

- Cut 1 strip 2½″ × width of fabric.

FROM ACCENT:

- Cut 2 strips 1½″ × width of fabric.

  Set aside 1 strip.

  From 1 strip, subcut 1 rectangle 1½″ × 21″.

CUTTING FOR 16″ BLOCKS

FROM FABRIC 1:

- Cut 1 strip 8½″ × width of fabric.
- Cut 1 strip 6½″ × width of fabric.

FROM FABRIC 2:

- Cut 1 strip 8½″ × width of fabric.

FROM FABRIC 3:

- Cut 1 strip 8½″ × width of fabric.

FROM FABRIC 4:

- Cut 2 strips 4½″ × width of fabric.

FROM ACCENT:

- Cut 3 strips 2½″ × width of fabric.

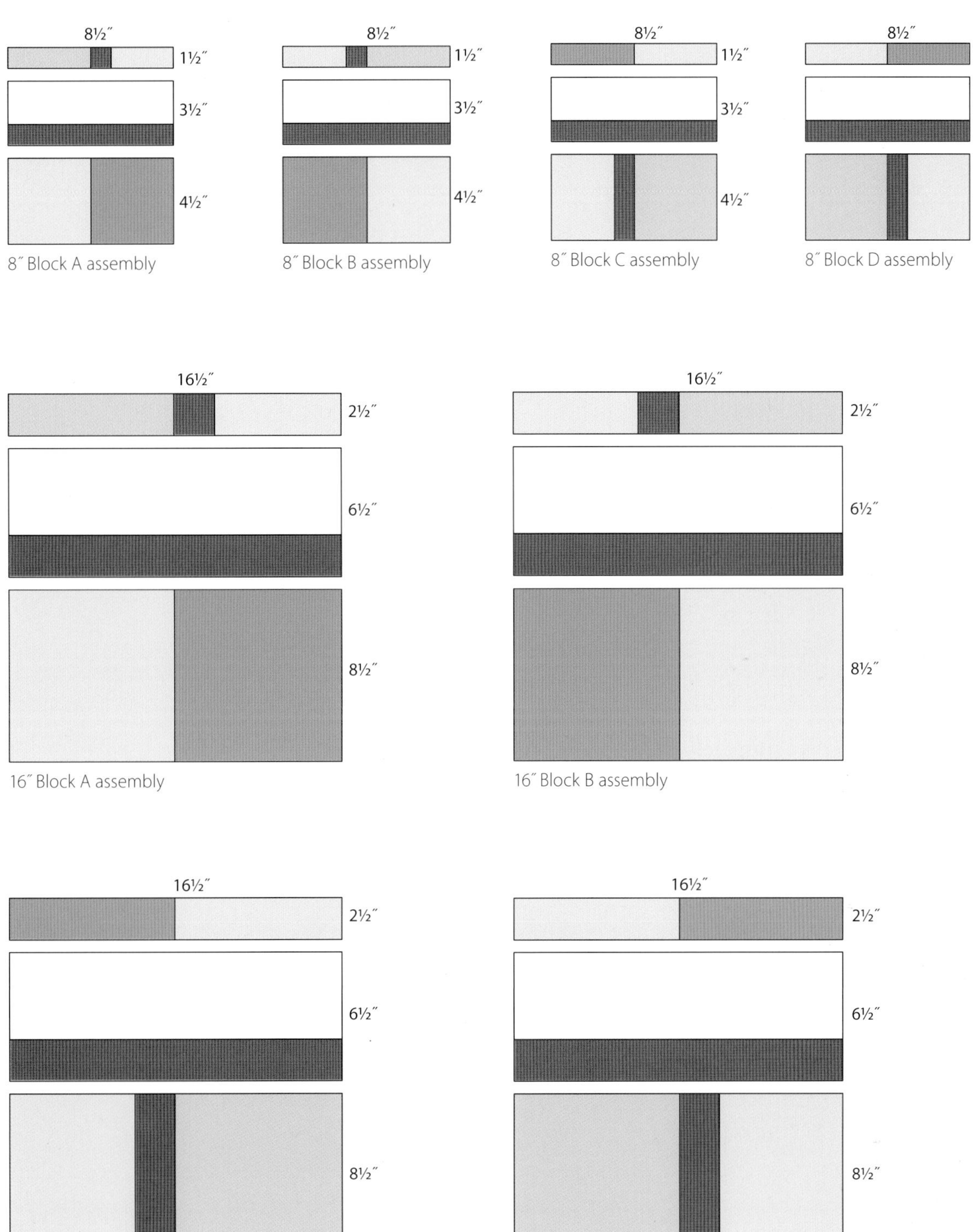

8″ Block A assembly

8″ Block B assembly

8″ Block C assembly

8″ Block D assembly

16″ Block A assembly

16″ Block B assembly

16″ Block C assembly

16″ Block D assembly

MAKE THE BLOCK

The first number in parentheses is for 8″ blocks; the second number is for 16″ blocks. The construction steps are the same for both sizes. Use ¼″ seams. Gently press all seams as you work. For a flat, finished look, press all seams open.

1. Sew the (4½″ × 21″, 8½″ × width of fabric) fabric 1 strip to the (4½″ × 21″, 8½″ × width of fabric) fabric 2 strip. This strip set will measure (8½″ × 21″, 16½″ × width of fabric).

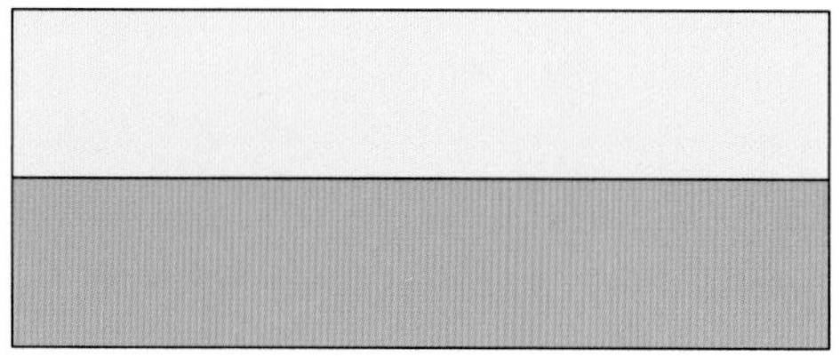

2. Subcut the 8½″ strip set into 2 segments at 4½″ intervals and 2 segments at 1½″ intervals. Subcut the 16½″ strip set into 2 segments at 8½″ intervals and 2 segments at 2½″ intervals.

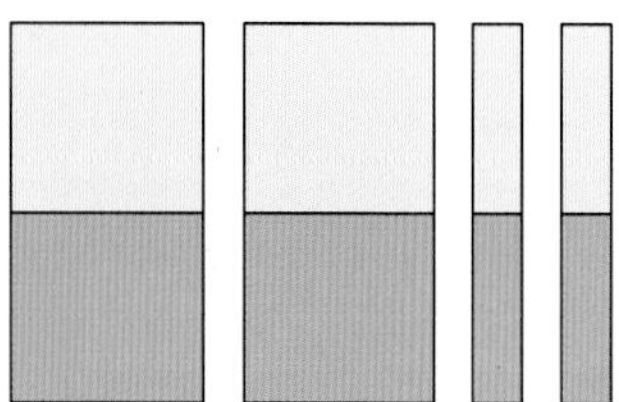

3. Sew the (3½″ × 21″, 6½″ × width of fabric) fabric 1 strip to the (1½″ × 21″, 2½″ × width of fabric) accent strip to the (4½″ × 21″, 8½″ × width of fabric) fabric 3 strip. This strip set will measure (8½″ × 21″, 16½″ × width of fabric).

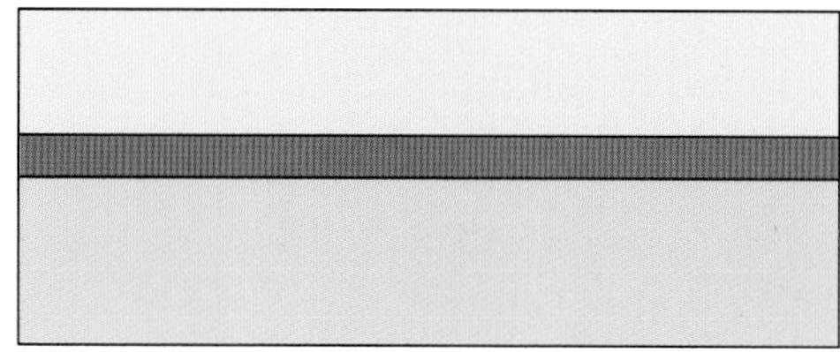

4. Subcut the 8½″ strip set into 2 segments at 4½″ intervals and 2 segments at 1½″ intervals. Subcut the 16½″ strip set into 2 segments at 8½″ intervals and 2 segments at 2½″ intervals.

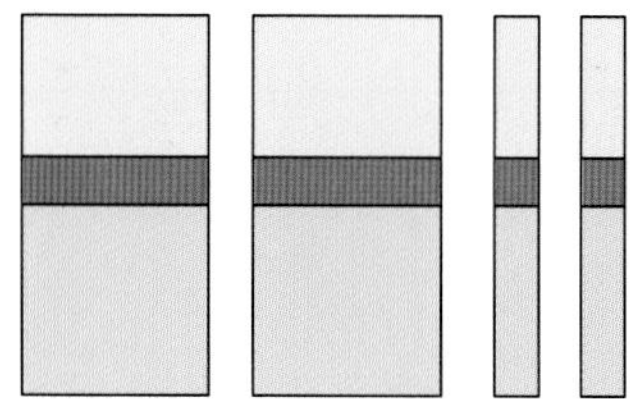

5. Sew the (1½″ × width of fabric, 2½″ × width of fabric) accent strip to the (2½″ × width of fabric, 4½″ × width of fabric) fabric 4 strip. If you are making 16″ blocks, sew 2 strip sets. This strip set will measure (3½″ × width of fabric, 6½″ × width of fabric).

6. Subcut 4 segments at (8½″, 16½″) intervals.

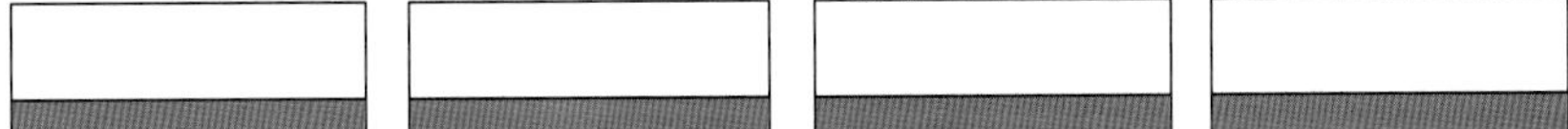

7. Arrange the segments from Steps 2, 4, and 6 to make 1 each of A, B, C, and D blocks. Sew the blocks in your desired arrangement.

ASSEMBLE THE PILLOW

Piece 4 blocks together in a 2 × 2 configuration.

Refer to Pillow with Overlapped Back (page 10) for instructions on finishing your pillow.

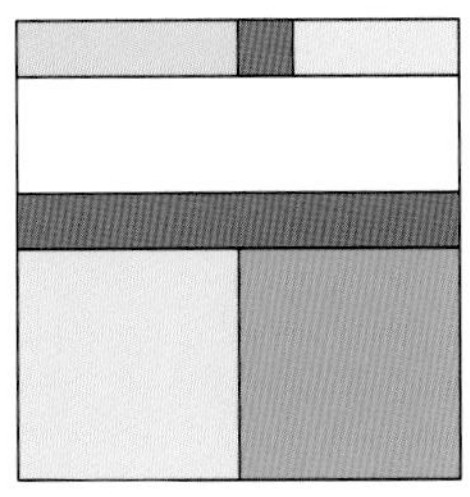

Block A

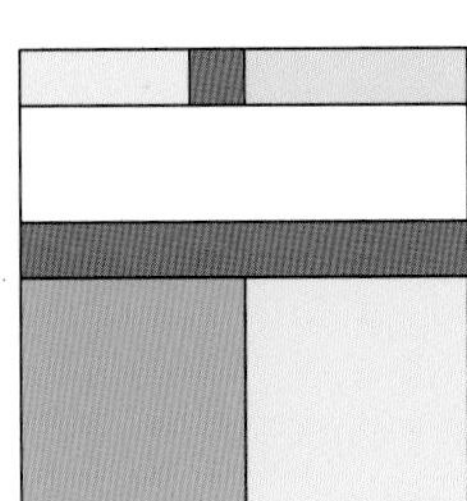

Block B

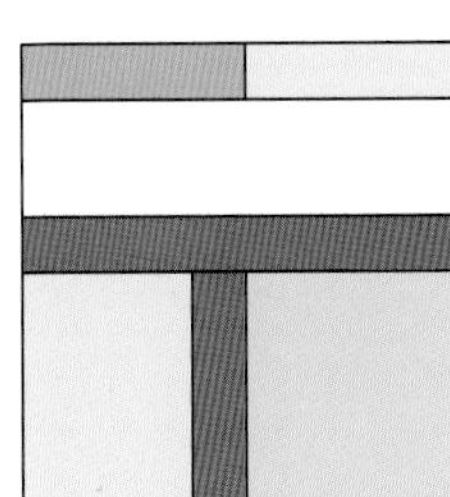

Block C

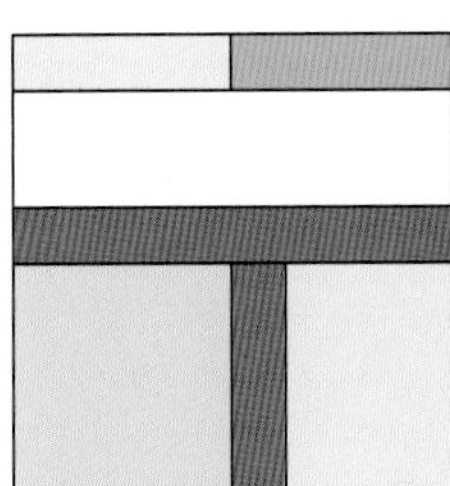

Block D

CRISPY WONTON BLOCK

CRISPY WONTON PILLOW, 16″ × 16″
MADE BY MARNY BUCK, 2014

The Crispy Wonton pillow is made from 8″ blocks, 2 A and 2 B.

Crispy Wonton is a deceptively simple, asymmetric block from which you can create a variety of shapes and patterns. It has both A and B orientations. Depending on the arrangement *you* choose, you might see negative space become the positive, links in a chain, zigzag lines, pseudo chevrons, and more.

Bottle Stoppers (page 52) in the Tasting Menu uses the 16″ block in a diagonal setting. *Éclairs* (page 102) in the Dessert Menu features the 8″ block in a grid setting.

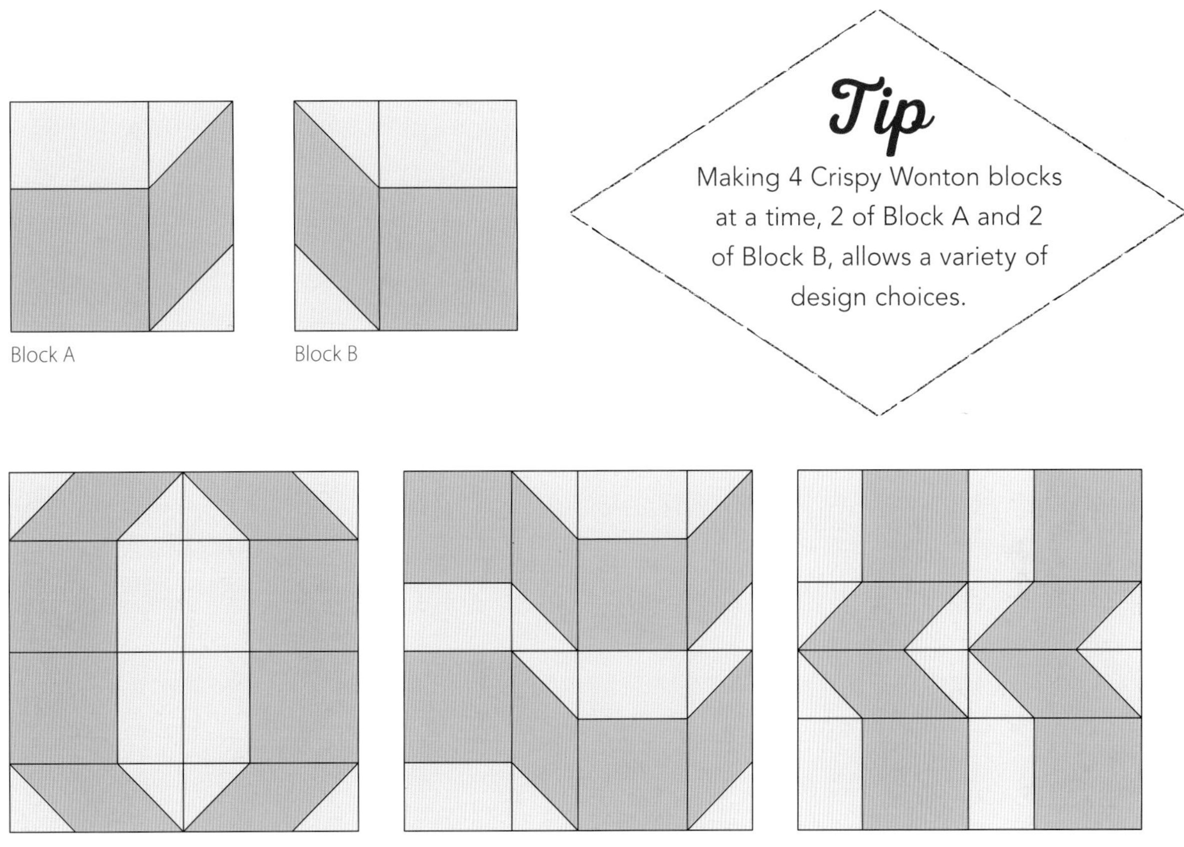

Block A
Block B
Tip
Making 4 Crispy Wonton blocks at a time, 2 of Block A and 2 of Block B, allows a variety of design choices.

Additional 4-block arrangements using 2 of Block A and 2 of Block B

CRISPY WONTON BLOCK RECIPE

Finished blocks: 8″ × 8″ (as shown in pillow) or 16″ × 16″

Ingredients

- **Color:** (⅓ yard (¾ yard)
- **Background:** ¼ yard (⅔ yard)

These yardages will make 4 blocks and are based on 42″ of usable width from nondirectional fabrics. These are minimum yardage requirements. You might choose to buy extra.

Prep the Ingredients

Cut all fabrics by the width of fabric. Remove selvages before cutting.

CUTTING FOR 8″ BLOCKS

FROM COLOR:

- Cut 1 strip 5½″ × width of fabric.
- Cut 1 strip 3½″ × width of fabric.

  Subcut 4 rectangles 3½″ × 8½″.

FROM BACKGROUND:

- Cut 2 strips 3½″ × width of fabric.

  Set aside 1 strip for strip set.

  From 1 strip, subcut 8 squares 3½″ × 3½″.

CUTTING FOR 16″ BLOCKS

FROM COLOR:

- Cut 1 strip 10½″ × width of fabric.
- Cut 2 strips 6½″ × width of fabric.

  Subcut 4 rectangles 6½″ × 16½″.

FROM BACKGROUND:

- Cut 3 strips 6½″ × width of fabric.

  Set aside 1 strip for strip set.

  From 2 strips, subcut 8 squares 6½″ × 6½″.

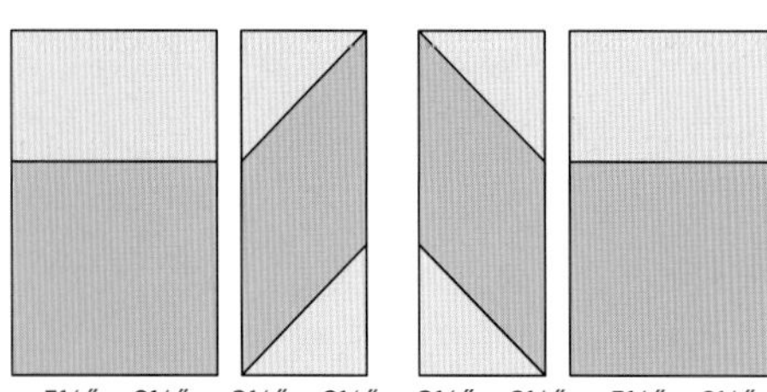

8″ Block A assembly

8″ Block B assembly

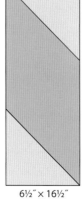

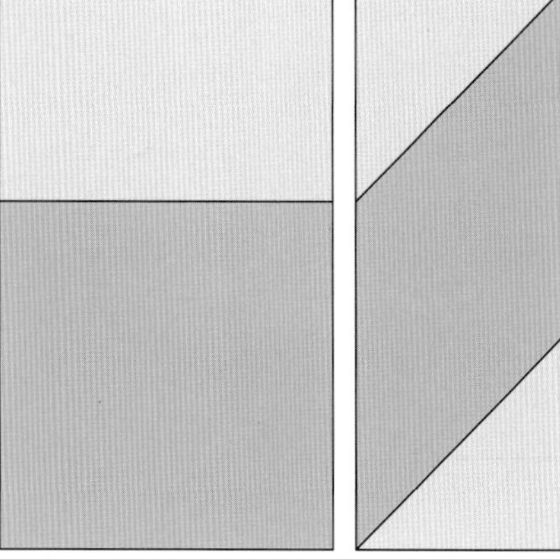

16″ Block A assembly

16″ Block B assembly

MAKE THE BLOCK

The first number in parentheses is for 8″ blocks; the second number is for 16″ blocks. The construction steps are the same for both sizes. Use ¼″ seams. Gently press all seams as you work, taking special care with any bias seams. For a flat, finished look, press all seams open.

1. Sew a (5½″, 10½″) color strip to a (3½″, 6½″) background strip.

2. Cut 4 segments at (5½″, 10½″) intervals.

3. Mark a diagonal line from corner to corner on the wrong side of each background square.

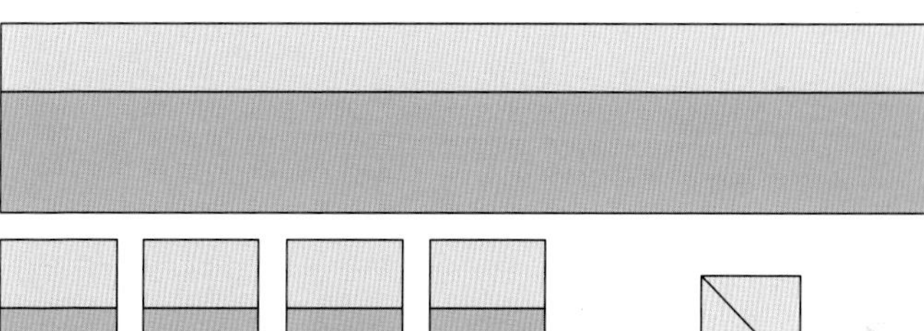

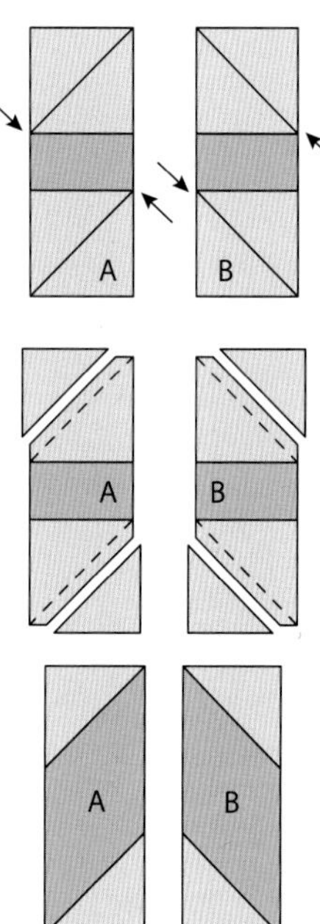

4. Arrange the marked background squares on both ends of the color rectangles, right sides together. Pay special attention to the orientation of the marked diagonals. Block A diagonals run from the lower left to the upper right. Block B diagonals run the opposite way, from the lower right to the upper left. Pin. Stitch on the marked diagonal lines.

> ***Tip***
>
> Start stitching the diagonal line at the arrows. The fabric will feed through your machine more easily!

5. Trim all thicknesses ¼″ from the diagonal stitching line. Be careful to trim on the correct side of the stitching line!

6. Press the remaining triangle to the right side.

7. Referring to block diagrams for orientation, sew the units together to make 4 blocks.

ASSEMBLE THE PILLOW

Piece 4 blocks together in a 2 × 2 configuration.

Refer to Pillow with Overlapped Back (page 10) for instructions on finishing your pillow.

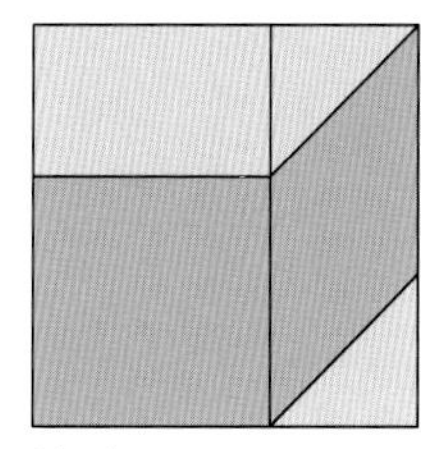

Block A

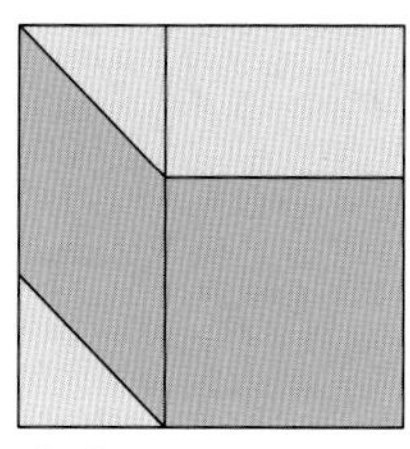

Block B

CELERY STICKS BLOCK

CELERY STICKS PILLOW, 28″ × 10″
MADE BY JILL GUFFY, 2014

The Celery Sticks pillow is made from 3 blocks—A, B, and C. The same configuration could be used to make a runner in 16″ blocks. Four of the 8″ blocks also could be combined to make a 16″ square pillow, using the setting options shown at the bottom of the next page.

Celery Sticks has three block formats, each with three staggered rectangles. Viewed vertically, Block A is asymmetrical and ascending; Block B is symmetrically concave or convex, depending on orientation; and Block C is asymmetrical and descending. These blocks may be turned 90° or 270° for horizontal orientation. The position of the positive elements within the negative space creates an active line or pattern.

Dippers (page 56) in the Tasting Menu shows the 8″ block, with added sashing, in a simple crossed vertical/horizontal setting. A combination of 16″ blocks and 8″ blocks is displayed in a staggered block setting in *Glycemic Index* (page 106) in the Dessert Menu.

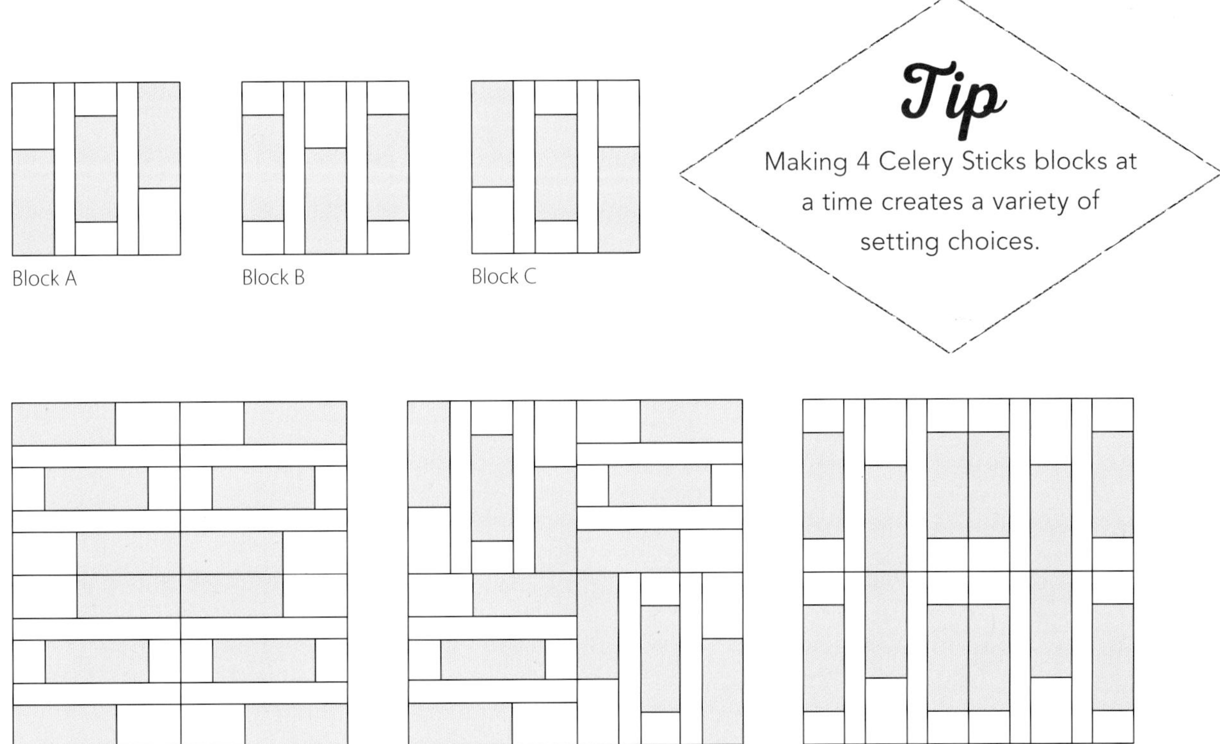

Block A
Block B
Block C
Tip
Making 4 Celery Sticks blocks at a time creates a variety of setting choices.

Additional 4-block arrangements using different combinations of blocks

CELERY STICKS BLOCK RECIPE

Finished blocks: 8″ × 8″ (as shown in pillow) or 16″ × 16″

Ingredients

These yardages will make 4 blocks and are based on 42″ of usable width from nondirectional fabrics. These are minimum yardage requirements. You might choose to buy extra.

- **Color:** ¼ yard (⅝ yard)
- **Background:** ⅓ yard for blocks plus ⅙ yard for pillow sashing (¾ yard for blocks plus ½ yard for runner sashing)
- **Backing:**

  Pillow backing: 28½″ × 10½″ (56½″ × 20½″)

  OR

  Runner backing: 37″ × 19″ (64″ × 29″)
- **Batting:** 37″ × 19″ (64″ × 29″)

Prep the Ingredients

Cut all fabrics by the width of fabric. Remove selvages before cutting.

CUTTING FOR 8″ BLOCKS

FROM COLOR:

- Cut 1 strip 5½″ × width of fabric.

  Subcut 2 rectangles 5½″ × 21″.

FROM BACKGROUND:

For blocks:

- Cut 1 strip 3½″ × width of fabric.

  Subcut 1 rectangle 3½″ × 21″.
- Cut 1 strip 2″ × width of fabric.

  Subcut 2 rectangles 2″ × 21″.
- Cut 2 strips 1½″ × width of fabric.

  Subcut 8 rectangles 1½″ × 8½″.

For sashing and border:

- Cut 3 strips 1½″ × width of fabric.

  Subcut 4 rectangles 1½″ × 8½″.

  Subcut 2 rectangles 1½″ × 28½″.

CUTTING FOR 16″ BLOCKS

FROM COLOR:

- Cut 2 strips 10½″ × width of fabric.

FROM BACKGROUND:

For blocks:

- Cut 1 strip 6½″ × width of fabric.
- Cut 2 strips 3½″ × width of fabric.
- Cut 4 strips 2½″ × width of fabric.

  Subcut 8 rectangles 2½″ × 16½″.

For sashing and border:

- Cut 5 strips 2½″ × width of fabric.

  From 2 strips, subcut 4 rectangles 2½″ × 16½″.

  Using 3 strips, piece and subcut 2 strips 2½″ × 56½″.

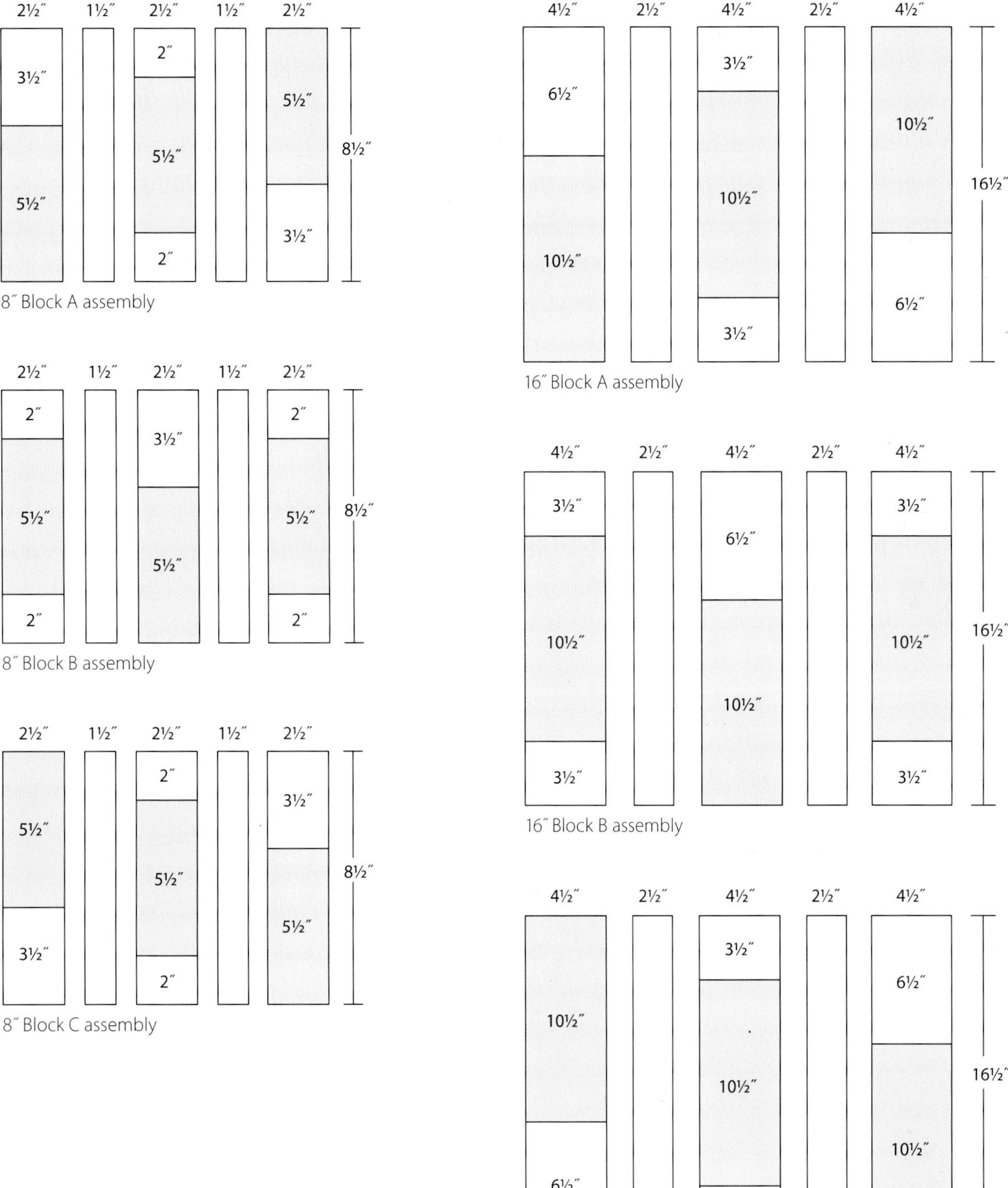

8″ Block A assembly

8″ Block B assembly

8″ Block C assembly

16″ Block A assembly

16″ Block B assembly

16″ Block C assembly

MAKE THE BLOCK

The first number in parentheses is for 8″ blocks; the second number is for 16″ blocks. The construction steps are the same for both sizes. Use ¼″ seams. Gently press all seams as you work. For a flat, finished look, press all seams open.

1. Sew a (5½″ × 21″, 10½″ × width of fabric) color strip to a (3½″ × 21″, 6½″ × width of fabric) background strip.

2. Cut 8 segments at (2½″, 4½″) intervals.

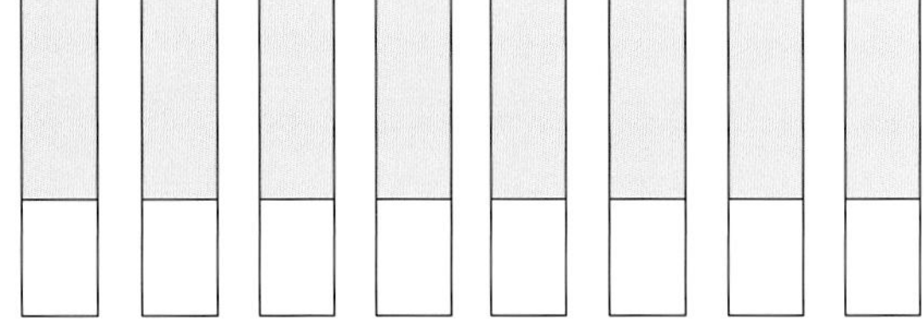

3. Sew a (2″ × 21″, 3½″ × width of fabric) background strip to each side of a (5½″ × 21″, 10½″ × width of fabric) color strip.

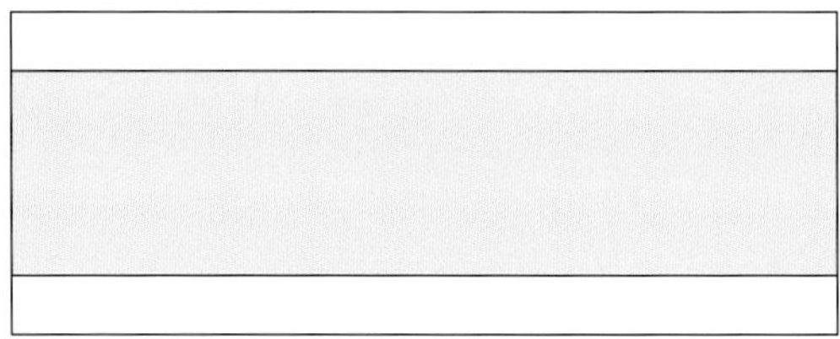

4. Cut 8 segments at (2½″, 4½″) intervals.

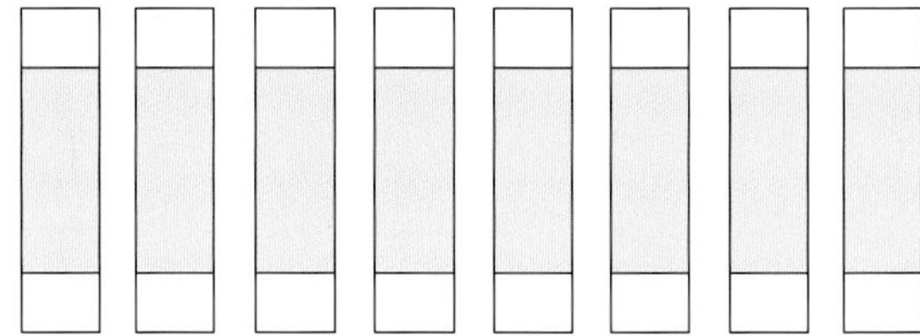

5. To make the blocks, sew Step 2 units, Step 4 units, and background rectangles (1½″ × 8½″, 2½″ × 16½″) following the block assembly diagrams. For the long pillow, make 1 each of A, B, and C blocks. There will be extra units.

ASSEMBLE THE PILLOW OR RUNNER

1. Arrange the blocks in A, B, C order. Sew 4 background sashing rectangles (1½″ × 8½″, 2½″ × 16½″) to the outside and between the blocks. These units measure (28½″ × 8½″, 56½″ × 16½″).

2. Sew a (28½″ × 1½″, 56½″ × 2½″) background border rectangle to the top and bottom. This 3-block unit measures (28½″ × 10½″, 56½″ × 20½″).

3. To make a pillow, refer to Pillow with Closed Back (page 10) for instructions. To make a runner, quilt and bind as if you were making a quilt. See Techniques (page 6) for information.

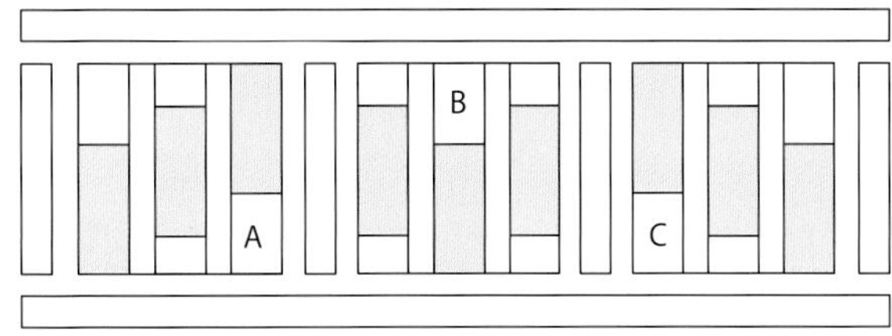

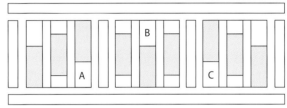

Pillow or runner assembly

Block A

Block B

Block C

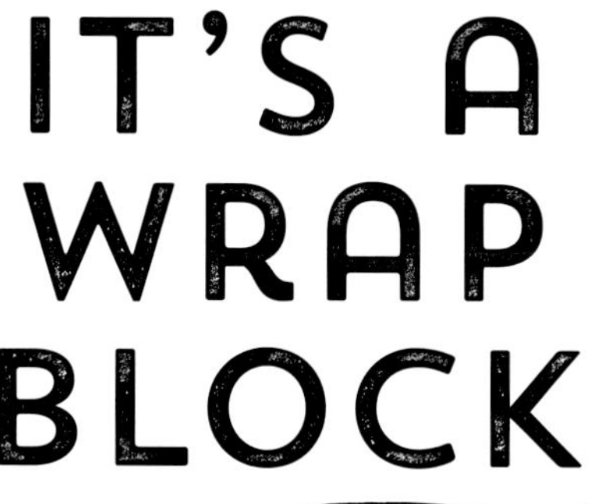

IT'S A WRAP PILLOW, 16″ × 16″
MADE BY JILL GUFFY, 2014

The It's a Wrap pillow uses 4 of the 5 color arrangements you can make from the same stack of squares.

It's a Wrap blocks start with a stack of five different fabric squares. Cut through all five layers and rearrange the pieces for varied color placement. The "wrap" effect occurs when two adjacent fabrics of the same color surround the corner of a central rectangle. The 8″ blocks start with five 9½″ squares, and the 16″ blocks start with five 17½″ squares. So 10″ precuts, fat quarters, and collections of fabrics are perfect for the layered cutting.

Mondrian Morsels (page 60) on the Tasting Menu features the 16″ block in the staggered setting. *Petits Fours* (page 112) in the Dessert Menu simplifies the design with an alternative horizontal setting.

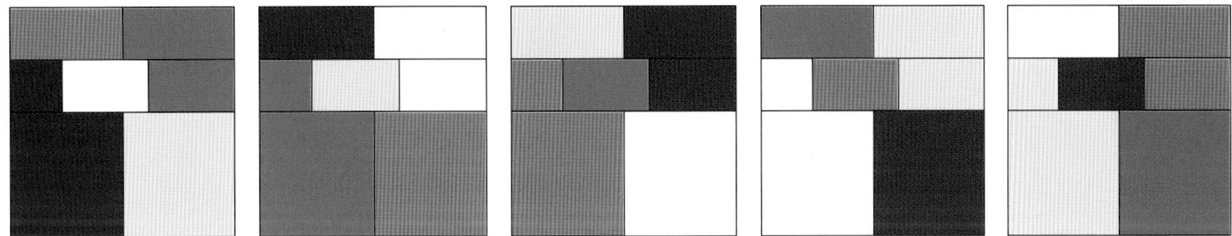

5 identical blocks with different color placement

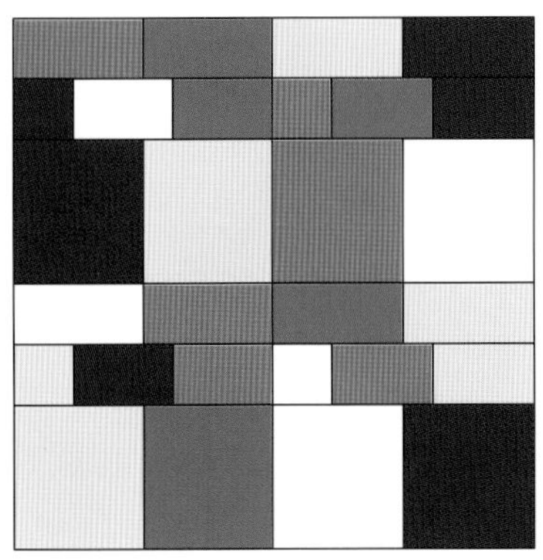

Arrangement ideas for 4 It's a Wrap blocks

IT'S A WRAP BLOCK RECIPE

Finished blocks: 8″ × 8″ (as shown in pillow) or 16″ × 16″

Ingredients

- **5 colors:** 9½″ × 9½″ square of each (17½″ × 17½″ square of each)

(If buying yardage, ⅓ yard (⅝ yard) will yield 4 (2) squares.)

Note

This process makes 5 blocks at a time. You will need 4 for the pillow and will have a leftover block. To plan a quilt using this block, divide the number of blocks you need by 5, rounding any fractions up to the next whole number. Multiply that number by the yardages listed in Ingredients.

These yardages will make 5 blocks and are based on 42″ of usable width from nondirectional fabrics. These are minimum yardage requirements. You might choose to buy extra.

Prep the Ingredients

The first number in parentheses is for 8″ blocks; the second number is for 16″ blocks.

Steps 1-3

1. Layer all 5 squares, right side up, directly on top of one another.

2. Starting on the left, cut a (2½″, 4½″) strip.

3. Cut another (2½″, 4½″) strip. A (4½″, 8½″) strip will remain.

4. Turn the stack 90° clockwise, maintaining the layers and the same order. Pull out the second row.

5. From the left, cut a (4½″, 8½′) strip from the first and third rows.

Cut another (4½″, 8½″) strip. Discard the remaining ½″.

6. From the left, cut a (2½″, 4½″) square from the second row.

Cut a strip (3½″, 6½″), leaving a (3½″, 6½″) piece.

7. Reassemble the rows in the original order. This ensures that any directional fabric will maintain the same orientation.

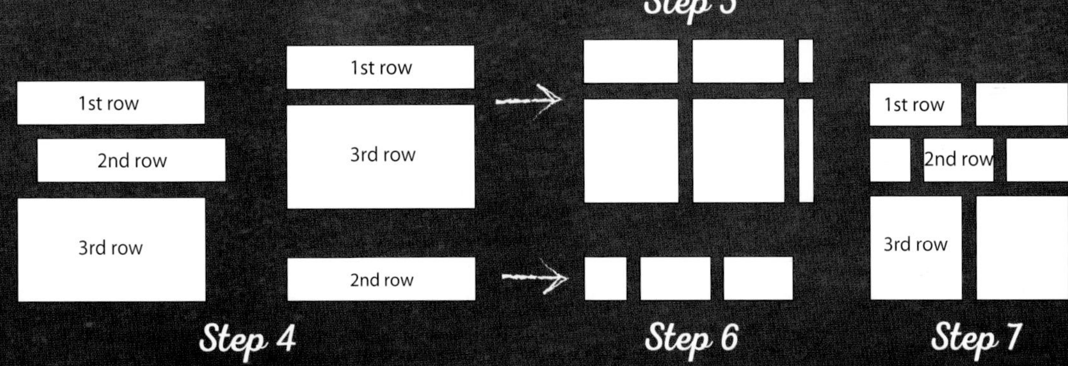

MAKE THE BLOCK

The construction steps are the same for both block sizes. Use ¼″ seams. Gently press all seams as you work. For a flat, finished look, press all seams open.

1. Following the shuffled block diagrams, rearrange the fabrics within each stack as follows:

- Row 1, rectangle on left: Leave stack as is.
- Rows 1 and 2, rectangles on right: Move top layer to the bottom of the stack.
- Row 3, squares on right: Move top 2 layers to the bottom of the stack.
- Rows 2 and 3, squares on left: Move top 3 layers to the bottom of the stack.
- Row 2 rectangle in center: Move top 4 layers to the bottom of the stack.

Five different fabrics should be visible on the top of your stack.

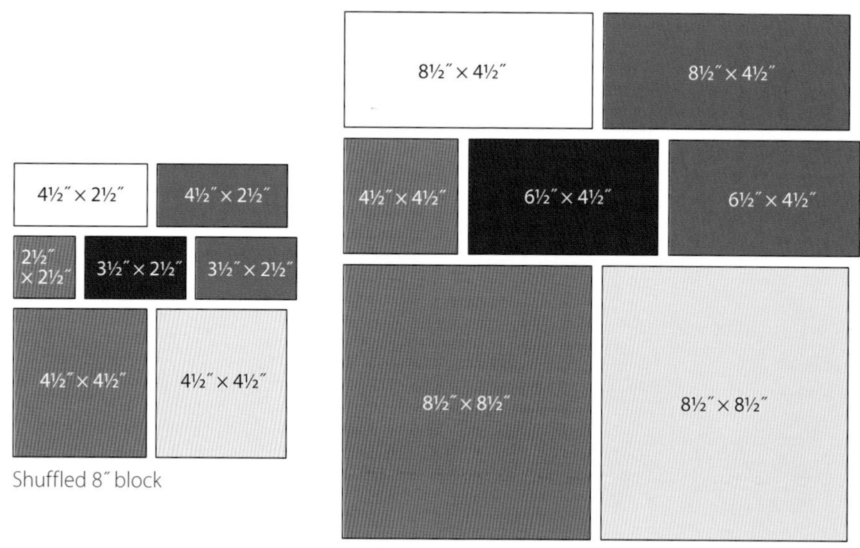

Shuffled 8″ block

Shuffled 16″ block

2. Move all stacks, maintaining the proper order, close to the sewing machine.

3. Working only with the top layer of pieces, sew the top row, the middle row, and the bottom row together in order.

4. Sew the rows together to complete the block.

5. The next block fabrics will be ready to sew in the same order. Make 5 blocks.

ASSEMBLE THE PILLOW

Piece 4 blocks together in a 2 × 2 configuration.

Refer to Pillow with Overlapped Back (page 10) for instructions on finishing your pillow.

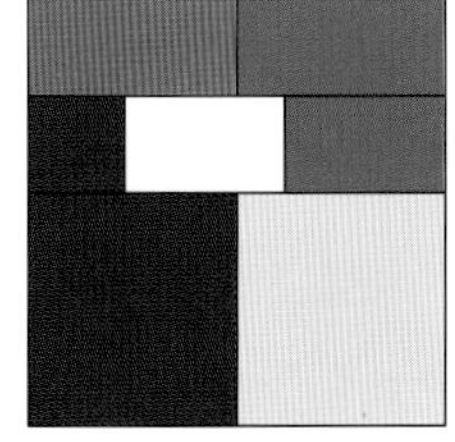
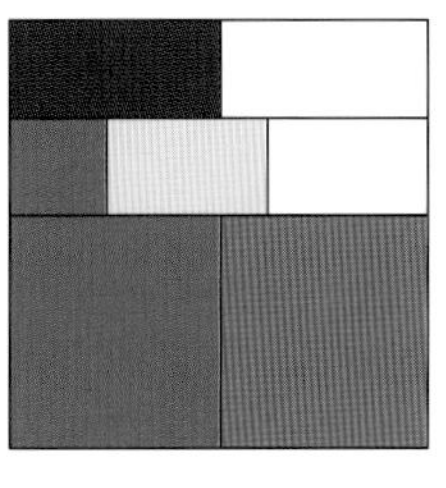
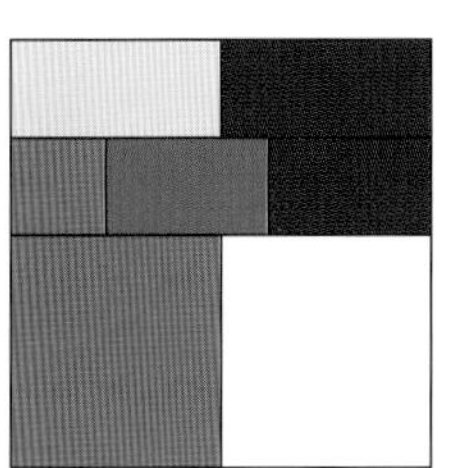
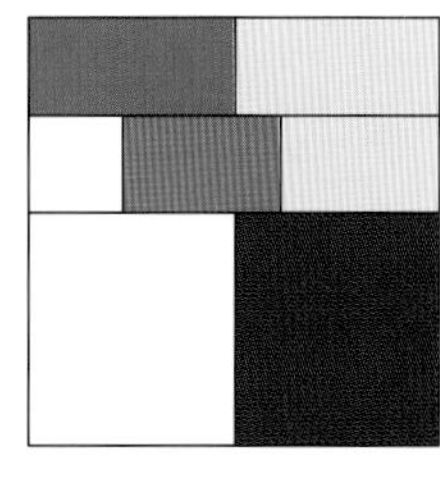
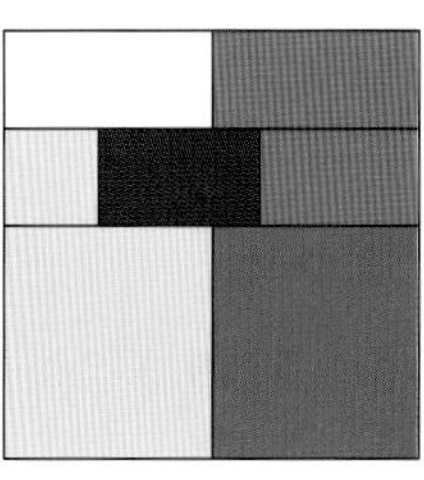

SUSHI BLOCK

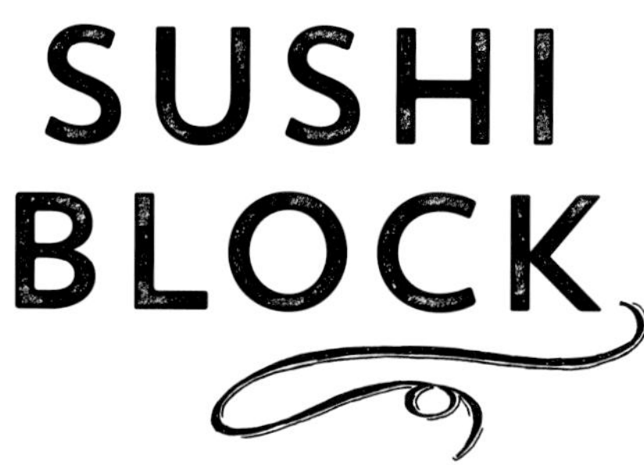

SUSHI PILLOW, 16″ × 16″
MADE BY MARNY BUCK, 2014

The Sushi pillow is made from 8″ blocks.

The Sushi block features an asymmetrically balanced modern rectangle. Depending on placement of the block within a setting, either restful or dynamic patterns can form.

Explore value with the Sushi block to create a delightful transparency, real or implied. The block is an opportunity to observe how two different values intersect to form a third. Here the rectangle is the lightest value, the extended arms are medium, and their intersection is darker. The background can be either the darkest or the lightest value, but a good contrast with the other three fabrics is required.

Spring Rolls shows 8″ blocks in a radiating setting in the Tasting Menu (page 64). The Sushi block takes on a different appearance in *Sweet Endings* (page 118) on the Dessert Menu. The structured diagonal setting causes blocks to interact with one another, forming rigid shapes and lines.

Sushi block

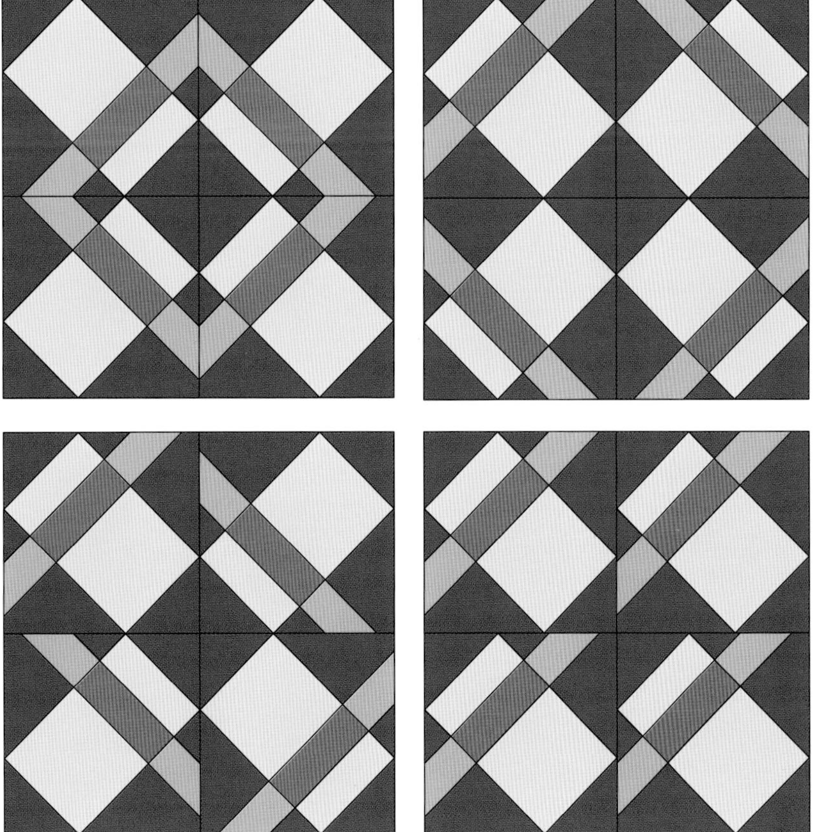

Additional ideas for 4-block arrangements

SUSHI BLOCK RECIPE

Finished block: 8″ × 8″ or 16″ × 16″

Ingredients

- **Light (yellow orange):** ¼ yard (½ yard)
- **Medium (orange):** ¼ yard (½ yard)
- **Dark (red orange):** ¼ yard (⅓ yard if nondirectional, ½ yard if directional)
- **Background (dark brown):** ½ yard (1¼ yards)

These yardages will make 4 blocks and are based on 42″ of usable width of fabric. Use a nondirectional fabric for the background; but the light, medium, and dark fabrics can be directional. The light, medium, and dark ingredient amounts may be good for one more recipe. Check before you multiply.

Prep the Ingredients

Cut all fabrics by the width of fabric unless otherwise stated. Remove selvages before cutting.

CUTTING FOR 8″ BLOCKS

FROM LIGHT:

- Cut 1 strip 6½″ × width of fabric.

  Subcut 4 rectangles 6½″ × 4¾″.

FROM MEDIUM:

- Cut 2 strips 5″ × the *length* of fabric to yield 2 rectangles 5″ × 9″.

FROM DARK:

- Cut 1 strip 4¾″ × the *length* of fabric to yield 1 rectangle 4¾″ × 9″.

FROM BACKGROUND:

- Cut 1 strip 7″ × width of fabric.

  Subcut 4 squares 7″ × 7″.

  Subcut each square once diagonally to yield 8 large triangles.

- Cut 1 strip 5″ × width of fabric.

  Subcut 4 squares 5″ × 5″.

  Subcut each square once diagonally to yield 8 small triangles.

CUTTING FOR 16″ BLOCKS

FROM LIGHT:

- Cut 1 strip 12″ × width of fabric.

  Subcut 4 rectangles 12″ × 9″.

FROM MEDIUM:

- Cut 2 strips 10″ × *length* of fabric to yield 2 rectangles 10″ × 18″.

FROM DARK:

- If *nondirectional* fabric, cut 1 strip 9″ × width of fabric.

  Subcut 1 rectangle 9″ × 18″.

- If *directional* fabric, cut 1 strip 9″ × *length* of fabric to yield 1 rectangle 9″ × 18″.

FROM BACKGROUND:

- Cut 2 strips 14″ × width of fabric.

  Subcut 4 squares 14″ × 14″.

  Subcut each square once diagonally to yield 8 large triangles.

- Cut 1 strip 10″ × width of fabric.

  Subcut 4 squares 10″ × 10″.

  Subcut each square once diagonally to yield 8 small triangles.

Using Stripes

It is fun to include stripes when exploring value. Cutting directions for Sushi blocks, *Spring Rolls* (page 64), and *Sweet Endings* (page 118) allow you to use stripes and all other directional fabrics in the light, medium, and dark positions. Cut the length of fabric parallel to selvage edges.

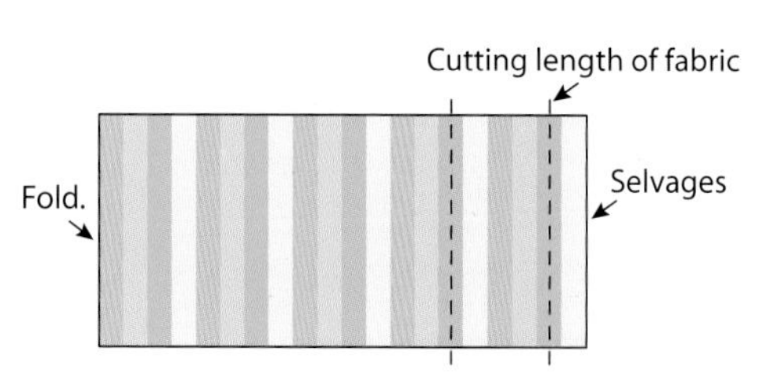

MAKE THE BLOCK

The first number in parentheses is for 8″ blocks; the second number is for 16″ blocks. Use ¼″ seams. Gently press all seams as you work, taking special care with any bias seams. For a flat, finished look, press all seams open.

1. Gently finger-press a fold at the center of the long sides of each light rectangle and the center of the long side of each large background triangle. Matching finger-pressed centers, sew the large triangles to the long sides of the light rectangles. Press gently.

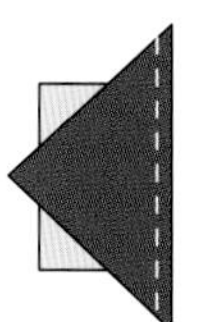

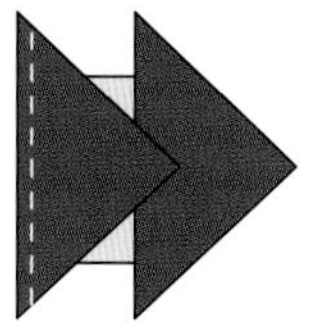

2. Rotate the block so that the rectangle is horizontal. Measure (2″, 3½″) from the right short end of the rectangle of the Step 1 unit. Use horizontal lines on the ruler to make sure the ruler remains square with the top and bottom. Cut and set aside.

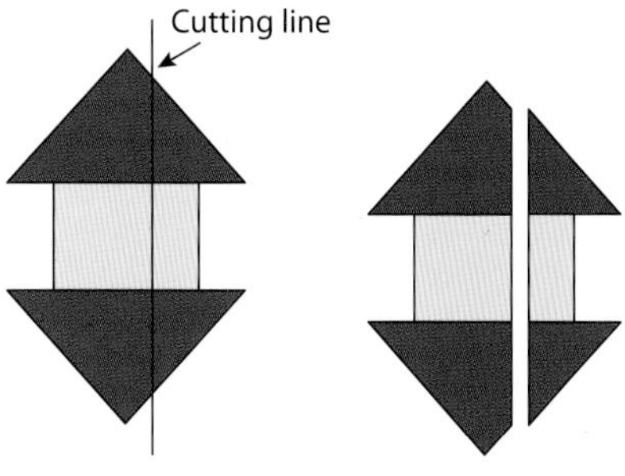

3. Sew a medium rectangle to each side of the dark rectangle, matching long sides.

4. Cut 4 segments from each strip set at (2″, 3½″) intervals.

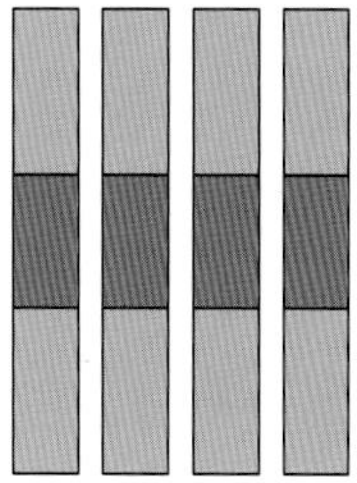

5. Match seams, pin, and sew a unit from Step 4 between the halves of each Step 2 unit.

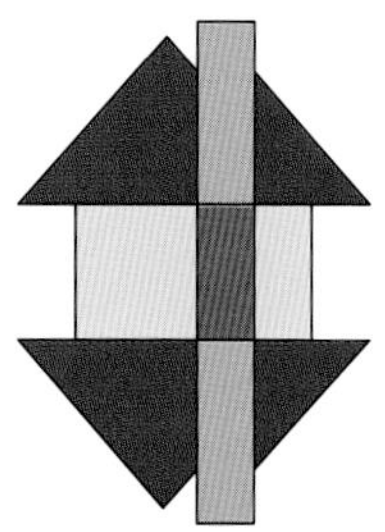

6. Carefully trim off only the excess "wings," keeping ruler square to the short edge of the light rectangle and to the horizontal seams in the block.

7. Gently finger-press the center of the short sides of the light rectangles within this unit and the long side of each small background triangle. Matching finger-pressed centers, sew the small triangles to the light rectangles.

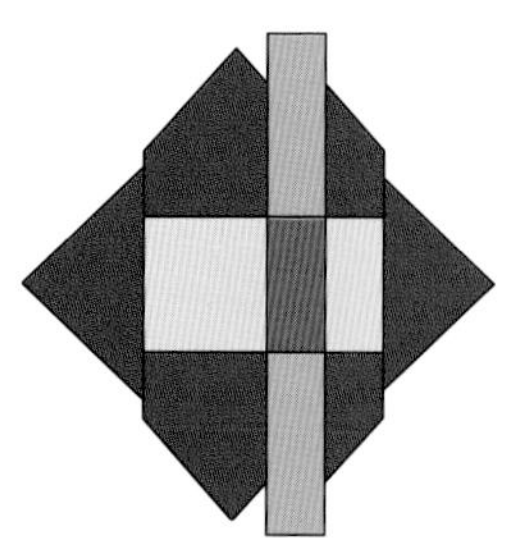

8. Rotate each block so that the internal rectangle is on a 45° diagonal. Trim to (8½″, 16½″) square, making sure the seam allowance is ¼″ at all 4 corners of the light rectangle and that the *raw* top and bottom of the block are square to the ruler for the first trim, and that the recently cut sides are square to the ruler for the second cut. Using these edges as guidelines as you trim ensures that the final blocks will match up perfectly with each other.

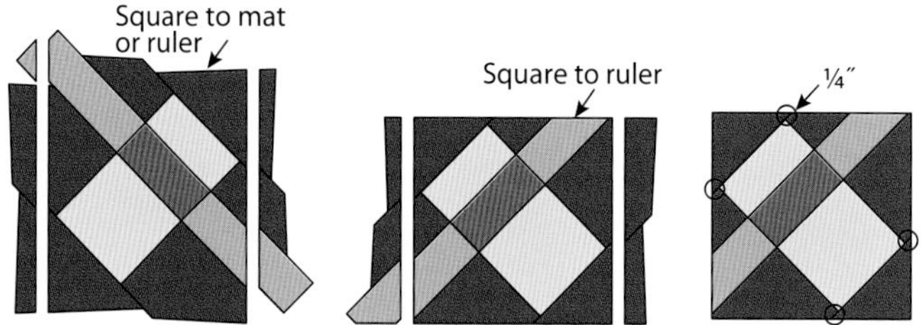

ASSEMBLE THE PILLOW

Piece 4 blocks together in a 2 × 2 configuration.

Refer to Pillow with Overlapped Back (page 10) for instructions on finishing your pillow.

Sushi block

TASTING MENU

QUILT PROJECTS TO SATISFY CRAVINGS

***Antipasto Platter* 44**
Crudités block • grid setting

***Snack Circuit* 48**
Salsa block • repeated horizontal setting

***Bottle Stoppers* 52**
Crispy Wonton block • diagonal setting

***Dippers* 56**
Celery Sticks block • horizontal/vertical/crossed setting

***Mondrian Morsels* 60**
It's a Wrap block • staggered setting

***Spring Rolls* 64**
Sushi block • radiating setting

A little taste of appetizers makes you hungry for a whole meal. Satisfy those cravings here with a tempting menu of projects. Each quilt project exhibits an Appetizer block (pages 11–42) in a selection from the Settings Menu (pages 69–88).

The Crudités block and grid setting make the Antipasto Platter quilt, perfect to share!

ANTIPASTO PLATTER

ntipasto Platter uses lively 8″ Crudités blocks in a structured grid setting. Simple geometric shapes scatter evenly across the surface of the quilt.

Silk cross-woven fabrics in eight colors shimmer on a warm, textured background.

Choose at least five colors that share similar intensities to make this and any polychromatic color scheme successful. One easy way to select colors is to combine primary, secondary, and tertiary hues from the color wheel. Here the hues work around the color wheel starting with yellow green, moving on to green, blue green, violet, red violet, red, red orange, and orange.

Simple quilting lines stream like ribbons from top to bottom down the quilt, providing an interesting texture while not competing with the exuberant array of color.

Binding with the background fabric allows the shapes and colors within the quilt to remain center stage.

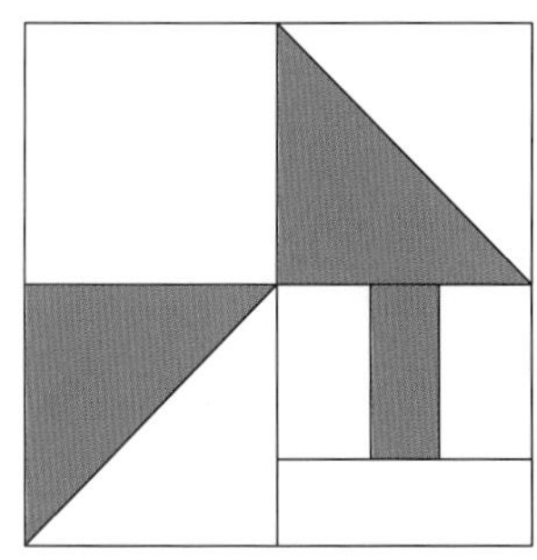

CRUDITÉS BLOCK + GRID SETTING

Finished quilt:	**Finished block:**	**Number of blocks:**
40½″ × 48½″	8″ × 8″	30

MAKE THE QUILT

Refer to the instructions for making 8″ blocks in Crudités Block Recipe (page 14).

1. Make 4 blocks of each color for 32 total. You need only 30 blocks for the quilt, but having the 2 extra blocks will help you make design decisions.

2. Referring to the quilt assembly diagram, arrange blocks into 5 columns of 6 blocks each, distributing color and shapes throughout the quilt.

3. Piece the blocks into columns.

4. Piece the columns together to complete the quilt top.

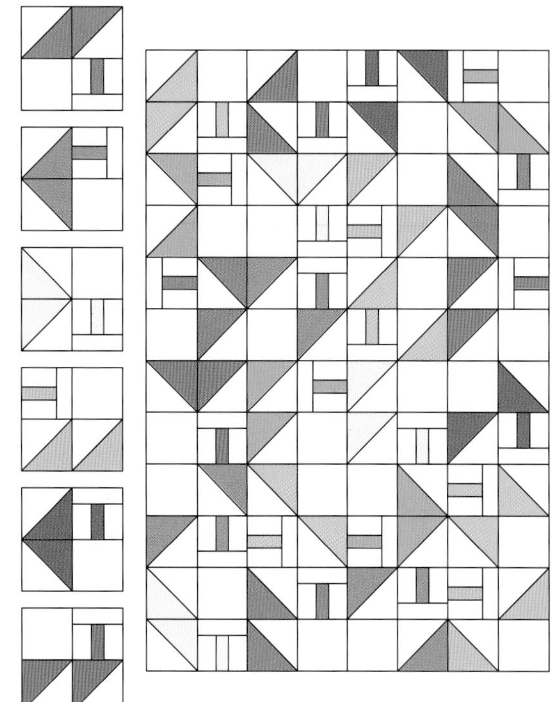

Quilt assembly

Ingredients

These yardages are based on 42″ of usable width from nondirectional fabrics.

- **8 colors:** ¼ yard each
- **Background:** 1⅞ yards
- **Binding:** ½ yard (We used the background fabric.)
- **Quilt backing:** 49″ × 57″
- **Batting:** 49″ × 57″

Prep the Ingredients

Cut all fabrics by the width of fabric. Remove selvages before cutting.

FROM EACH COLOR:

- Cut 1 strip 5″ × width of fabric.

  Subcut 4 squares 5″ × 5″.

  Subcut 1 strip 1½″ × 21″.

FOR BINDING:

- Cut 5 strips 2½″ × width of fabric.

FROM BACKGROUND:

- Cut 4 strips 5″ × width of fabric.

  Subcut 32 squares 5″ × 5″.
- Cut 4 strips 4½″ × width of fabric.

  Subcut 32 squares 4½″ × 4½″.
- Cut 8 strips 2″ × width of fabric.

  Subcut each at the fold for strip sets.
- Cut 4 strips 1¾″ × width of fabric.

  Subcut 32 rectangles 1¾″ × 4½″.

Antipasto Platter, 40½″ × 48½″, made by Marny Buck, machine quilted by April West using the Streamers pantograph by Norma Woods Sharp, 2014

SNACK CIRCUIT

Snack Circuit resembles a computer circuit board, using all four Salsa blocks rotated to create various juxtapositions. In this design, some of the lines and squares in the blocks become different shapes.

Negative space between the strips is a feature of this horizontal setting and occasionally allows the negative space within the block to "bleed" into the background. The message is broken but not lost; the eye can read the pattern. A full range of solid values makes this quilt graphic.

The complementary coral and aqua color scheme is a modern interpretation of the traditional orange and blue. The coral is the warmest, most saturated hue and therefore used as the accent next to the cool aqua and white. Neutrals add to the interest and balance the color. The darker values ground the design. Shapes, color, value, and negative space create this simple but complex statement.

Neutral quilting thread adds background definition. The casual, rounded square shapes highlight the colors with just a little more contrast. It is sophisticated modern. Dark aqua binding reinforces the colors within the quilt. The final edge wraps it into a happy package.

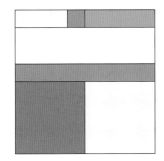

SALSA BLOCK + REPEATED HORIZONTAL SETTING

Finished quilt:	**Finished block:**	**Number of blocks:**
48½″ × 64½″	8″ × 8″	19

Ingredients

These yardages are based on 42″ of usable width from nondirectional fabrics.

- **Light aqua:** ⅞ yard
- **Medium gray:** ½ yard
- **Coral:** ½ yard
- **Dark aqua:** ½ yard
- **Cream:** 2⅜ yards
- **Binding:** ½ yard (We used dark aqua.)
- **Quilt backing:** 57″ × 73″
- **Batting:** 57″ × 73″

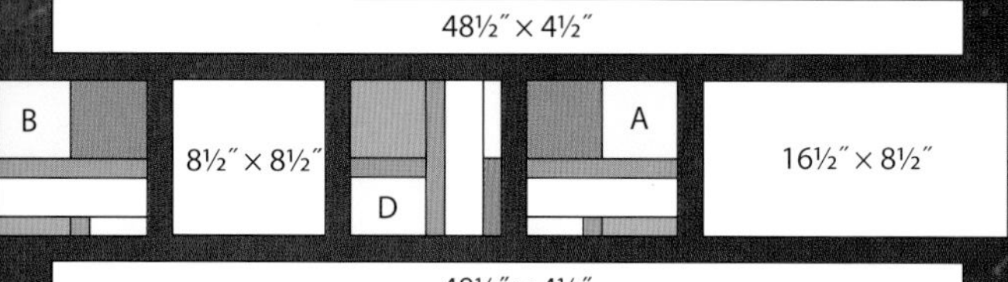

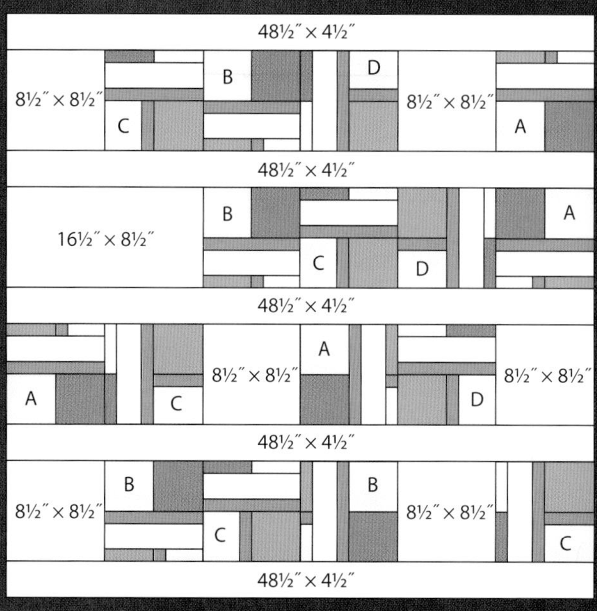

Quilt assembly

Prep the Ingredients

Cut all fabrics by the width of fabric. Remove selvages before cutting.

FROM LIGHT AQUA:

- Cut 3 strips 4½″ × width of fabric.
- Cut 3 strips 3½″ × width of fabric.

FROM MEDIUM GRAY:

- Cut 3 strips 4½″ × width of fabric.

FROM CORAL:

- Cut 9 strips 1½″ × width of fabric.

FROM DARK AQUA:

- Cut 3 strips 4½″ × width of fabric.

FOR THE BINDING:

- Cut 6 strips 2½″ × width of fabric.

FROM CREAM:

For blocks:

- Cut 6 strips 2½″ × width of fabric.

For quilt setting pieces:

- Cut 3 strips 8½″ × width of fabric.

  Subcut 2 rectangles 8½″ × 16½″.

  Subcut 7 squares 8½″ × 8½″.

- Cut 8 strips 4½″ × width of fabric.

  Subcut 6 rectangles 4½″ × 41″.

  Subcut 6 rectangles 4½″ × 8″.

  Stitch each 41″ rectangle to an 8″ rectangle to yield sashing strips 4½″ × 48½″.

MAKE THE QUILT

Refer to the instructions for making 8″ blocks in Salsa Block Recipe (page 18).

1. Make 3 Step 1 strip sets of light aqua (4½″) and medium gray. Cut 12 segments at 4½″ intervals and 12 segments at 1½″ intervals.

2. Make 3 Step 2 strip sets of light aqua (3½″), coral, and dark aqua. Cut 12 segments at 4½″ intervals and 12 segments at 1½″ intervals.

3. Make 6 Step 3 strip sets of coral and cream. Cut 24 segments at 8½″ intervals.

4. Arrange the segments to make 6 each of A, B, C, and D blocks for 24 total. You need only 19 blocks, but having the extra 5 blocks can help you make design decisions.

5. Referring to the quilt assembly diagram, arrange and piece the blocks and background pieces in 5 horizontal rows, with long sashing strips between each row and at the top and bottom of the quilt.

6. Sew the rows together to complete the quilt top.

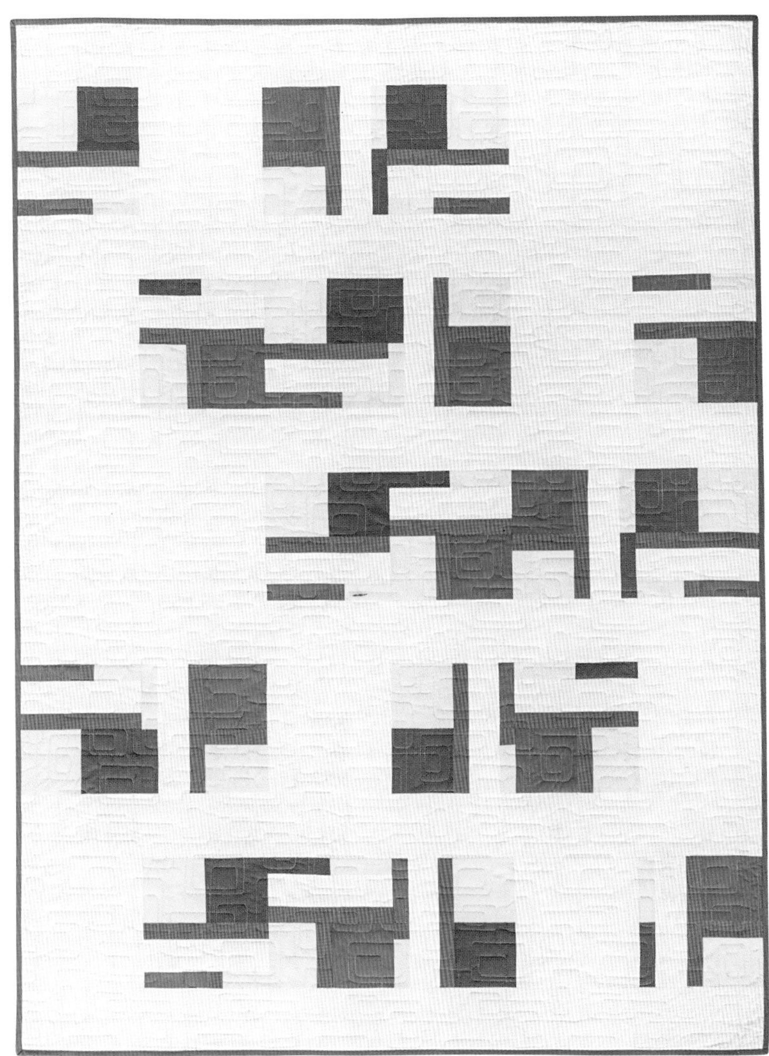

Snack Circuit, 48½″ × 64½″, made by Jill Guffy, machine quilted by April West with the Bauhaus pantograph by Urban Elementz, 2014

BOTTLE STOPPERS

ottle Stoppers uses hard-edged geometric 16″ Crispy Wonton blocks in an active diagonal setting. Large, overlapping shapes dominate the quilt.

Five fabrics in a variety of hues and values move from shape to shape, creating the implied overlap and the illusion of depth. The warm, dull gray background and the tinted yellow green are a perfect foil to the toned and spicy orange, red-orange, violet, and red-violet hues.

Quilting lines are reminiscent of simplified Moroccan tiles. Choosing a motif common to North Africa goes hand in hand with the spice-filled color scheme.

We chose binding with background fabric so the oversized colorful shapes would remain the focus.

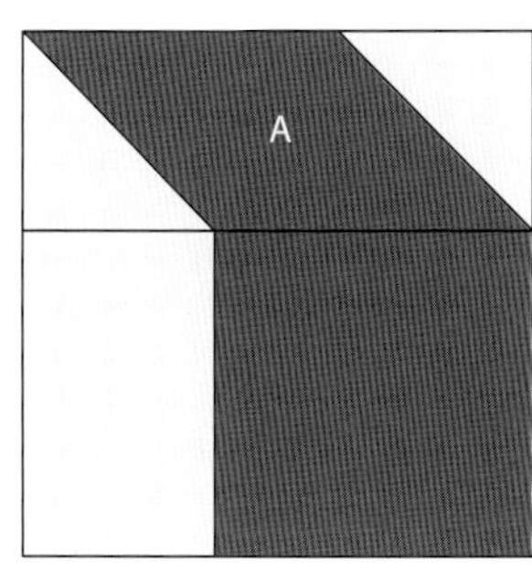

CRISPY WONTON BLOCK + DIAGONAL SETTING

Finished quilt:	Finished block:	Number of blocks:
96½″ × 96½″	16″ × 16″	16

MAKE THE QUILT

Refer to the instructions for making 16″ blocks in Crispy Wonton Block Recipe (page 24).

1. Make 2 of Block A and 2 of Block B from red violet.

2. Make 2 of Block A and 1 of Block B from each of the remaining colors—violet, orange, red orange, and yellow green.

3. Referring to the quilt assembly diagram, arrange and sew the blocks and background pieces into 6 columns.

4. Sew the columns together to complete the quilt top.

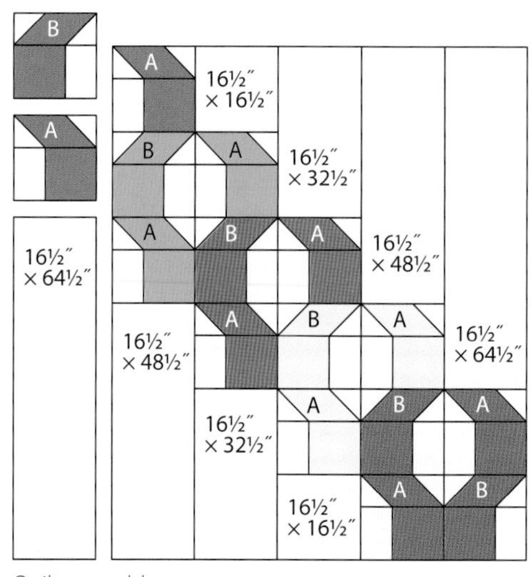

Quilt assembly

Ingredients

These yardages are based on 42″ of usable width from nondirectional fabrics.

- **Color fabrics:** ¾ yard each of 5 colors
- **Background:** 2¼ yards for blocks plus 4⅜ yards for quilt setting pieces
- **Binding:** ⅞ yard (We used the background fabric.)
- **Quilt backing:** 105″ × 105″
- **Batting:** 105″ × 105″

Prep the Ingredients

Cut all fabrics by the width of fabric. Remove selvages before cutting.

FROM EACH VIOLET, ORANGE, RED ORANGE, AND YELLOW GREEN:

- Cut 1 strip 10½″ × width of fabric.
- Cut 2 strips 6½″ × width of fabric.

  Subcut 3 rectangles 6½″ × 16½″.

FROM RED VIOLET:

- Cut 1 strip 10½″ × width of fabric.
- Cut 2 strips 6½″ × width of fabric.

  Subcut 4 rectangles 6½″ × 16½″.

FOR BINDING:

- Cut 11 strips 2½″ × width of fabric.

FROM BACKGROUND:

For blocks:

- Cut 11 strips 6½″ × width of fabric.

  Subcut 6 strips into 32 squares 6½″ × 6½″.

For quilt setting pieces:

- Cut 9 strips 16½″ × width of fabric.

  From 1 strip, subcut 2 squares 16½″ × 16½″.

  From each of 2 strips, subcut a rectangle 16½″ × 32½″.

  Using 4 strips, piece and subcut 2 rectangles 16½″ × 64½″.

  Using 2 strips and the remaining partial strips, piece and subcut 2 strips 16½″ × 48½″.

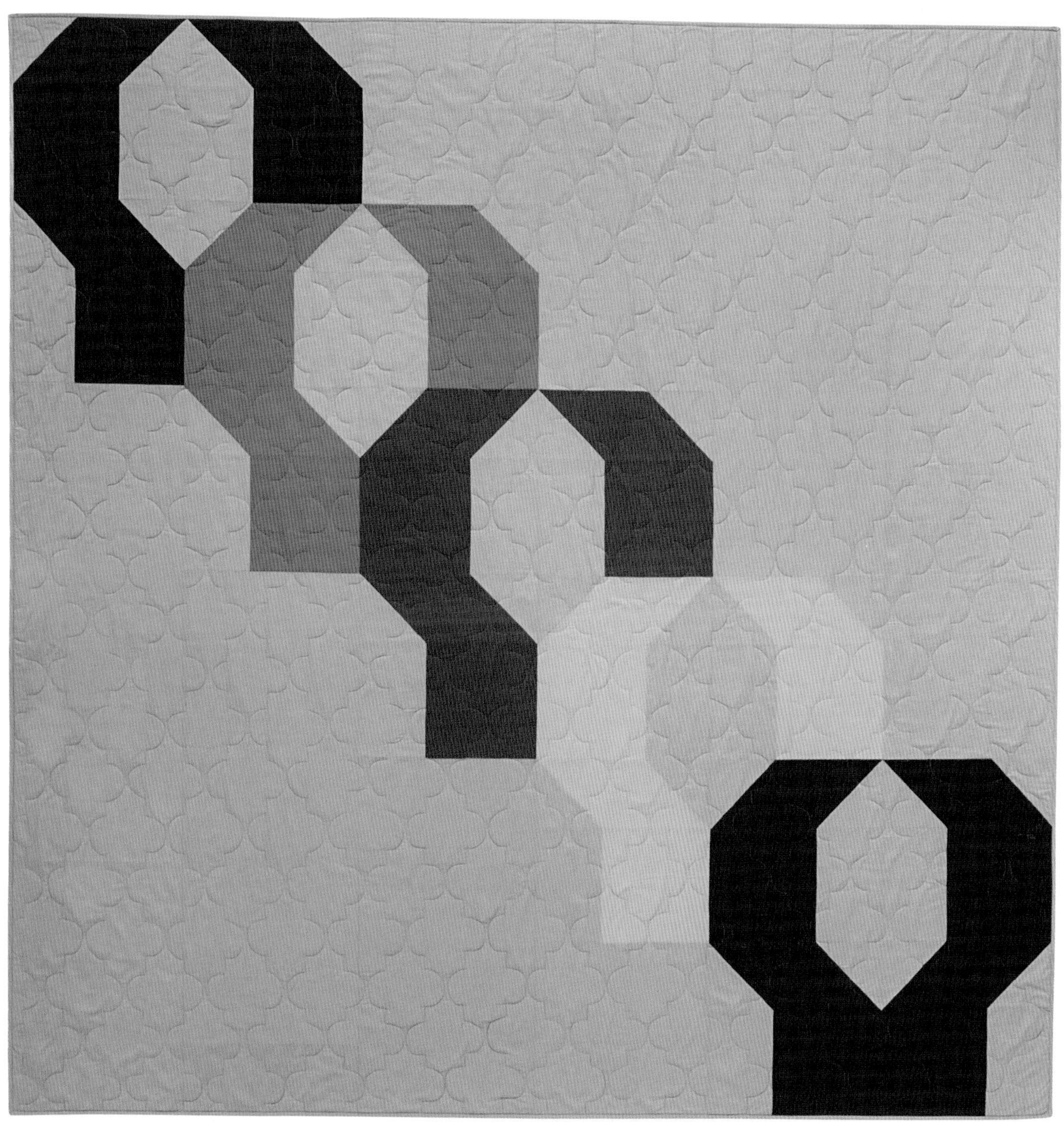

Bottle Stoppers, 96½″ × 96½″, made by Marny Buck, machine quilted by April West in a custom design referencing Moroccan tile, 2014

DIPPERS

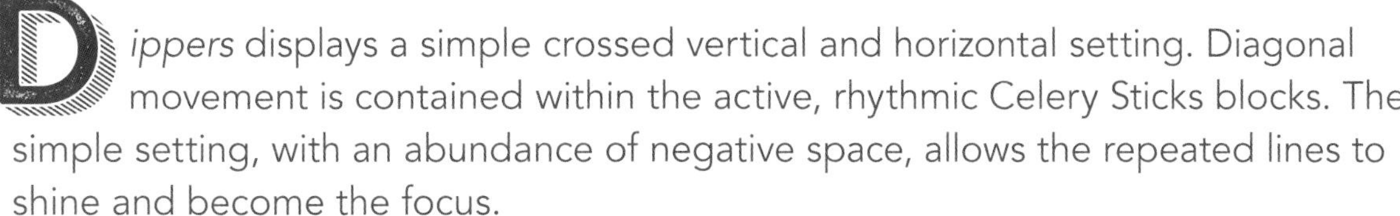

Dippers displays a simple crossed vertical and horizontal setting. Diagonal movement is contained within the active, rhythmic Celery Sticks blocks. The simple setting, with an abundance of negative space, allows the repeated lines to shine and become the focus.

Choosing an analogous scheme makes fabric selection easy. Side-by-side hues on the color wheel ensure fair play. Dull versus saturated and a variety in value adds interest. Blues and greens, one of nature's finest combinations, are always soothing and pleasing to the eye.

The simple coiled quilting pattern softens the straight-line edges. The thread color melts into the background so as not to compete with the focus, giving the quilt more dimensional interest.

Binding decisions vary with the functionality of the quilt. *Dippers* is perfect for a wall quilt, so the binding edge also melts into the background. As a functional throw, a medium-value edge would be more colorful and forgiving.

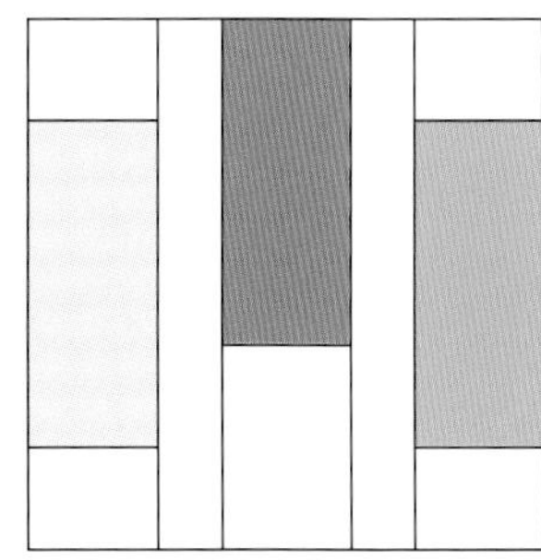

CELERY STICKS BLOCK + CROSSED VERTICAL/HORIZONTAL SETTING

Finished quilt:	Finished block:	Number of blocks:
55½″ × 73½″	8″ × 8″	13

Ingredients

These yardages are based on 42″ of usable width from nondirectional fabrics.

- **7 colors:** ¼ yard each of analogous colors in a variety of values, mostly medium with 1 or 2 lights and 1 or 2 darks
- **Background:** 1⅜ yards for blocks plus 2⅞ yards for quilt setting pieces
- **Binding:** ⅝ yard (We used the background.)
- **Quilt backing:** 64″ × 82″
- **Batting:** 64″ × 82″

Tip

Individual scrappy fabrics work well for the color in the Celery Sticks blocks. Follow the background ingredient amounts given in Celery Sticks Block Recipe (page 28) for the number of blocks you choose to make. Cut colors and background fabrics individually and piece as described in Prep the Ingredients (page 108) and Make the Quilt (page 110) for *Glycemic Index*.

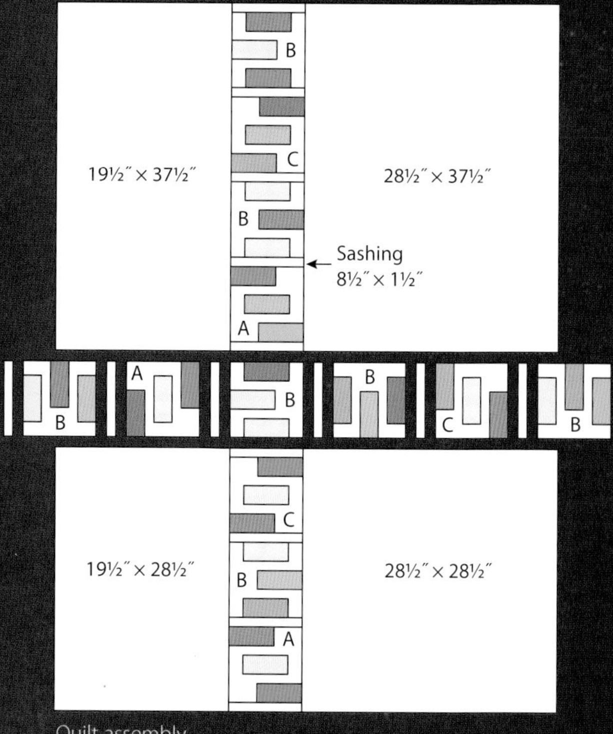

Quilt assembly

Prep the Ingredients

Cut all fabrics by the width of fabric. Remove selvages before cutting.

FROM EACH COLOR:

- Cut 5½″ × width of fabric.

  Subcut 2 rectangles 5½″ × 21″.

FOR BINDING:

- Cut 7 strips 2½″ × width of fabric.

FROM BACKGROUND:

For blocks and sashing:

- Cut 4 strips 3½″ × width of fabric.

  Subcut 7 rectangles 3½″ × 21″.
- Cut 7 strips 2″ × width of fabric.

  Subcut 14 rectangles 2″ × 21″.
- Cut 2 strips 8½″ × width of fabric.

  Subcut 42 rectangles 1½″ × 8½″.

For quilt setting pieces:

- Cut 2 strips 19½″ × width of fabric.

  Subcut 1 rectangle 19½″ × 37½″.

  Subcut 1 rectangle 19½″ × 28½″.
- Cut 2 strips 28½″ × width of fabric.

  Subcut 1 square 28½″ × 28½″.

  Subcut 1 rectangle 28½″ × 37½″.

MAKE THE QUILT

Refer to the instructions for making 8″ blocks in Celery Sticks Block Recipe (page 28).

1. For each color, sew a 5½″ × 21″ color rectangle to a 3½″ × 21″ background rectangle.

2. Cut 7 segments from each at 2½″ intervals.

3. Sew a 2″ × 21″ background rectangle to each side of the 7 remaining 5½″ × 21″ color rectangles. These 7 strip sets will measure 8½″ × 21″.

4. Cut 7 segments from each at 2½″ intervals.

5. This pattern uses 13 blocks: 3 A, 7 B, and 3 C. Before you sew each block together, preview the color arrangement on a design wall by alternating Step 1 and Step 2 segments, turning for the correct orientation and a pleasing color distribution. There will be extra segments to help with design decisions.

6. Sew each block together. Referring to the quilt assembly diagram, sew background sashing strips between the blocks to make 1 pieced vertical column and 2 shorter pieced horizontal rows. Stitch the short horizontal pieced rows between the larger pieces of quilt background fabric to make 2 more columns.

7. Stitch the columns together to complete the quilt top.

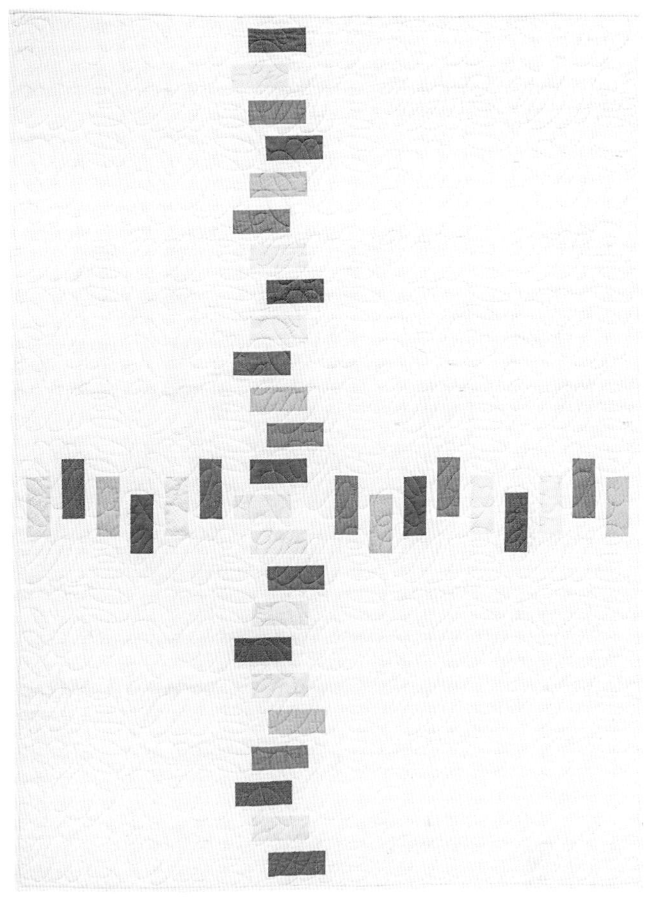

Dippers, 55½″ × 73½″, made by Jill Guffy, machine quilted by April West using the Coil pantograph by Timeless Quilting Designs, 2014

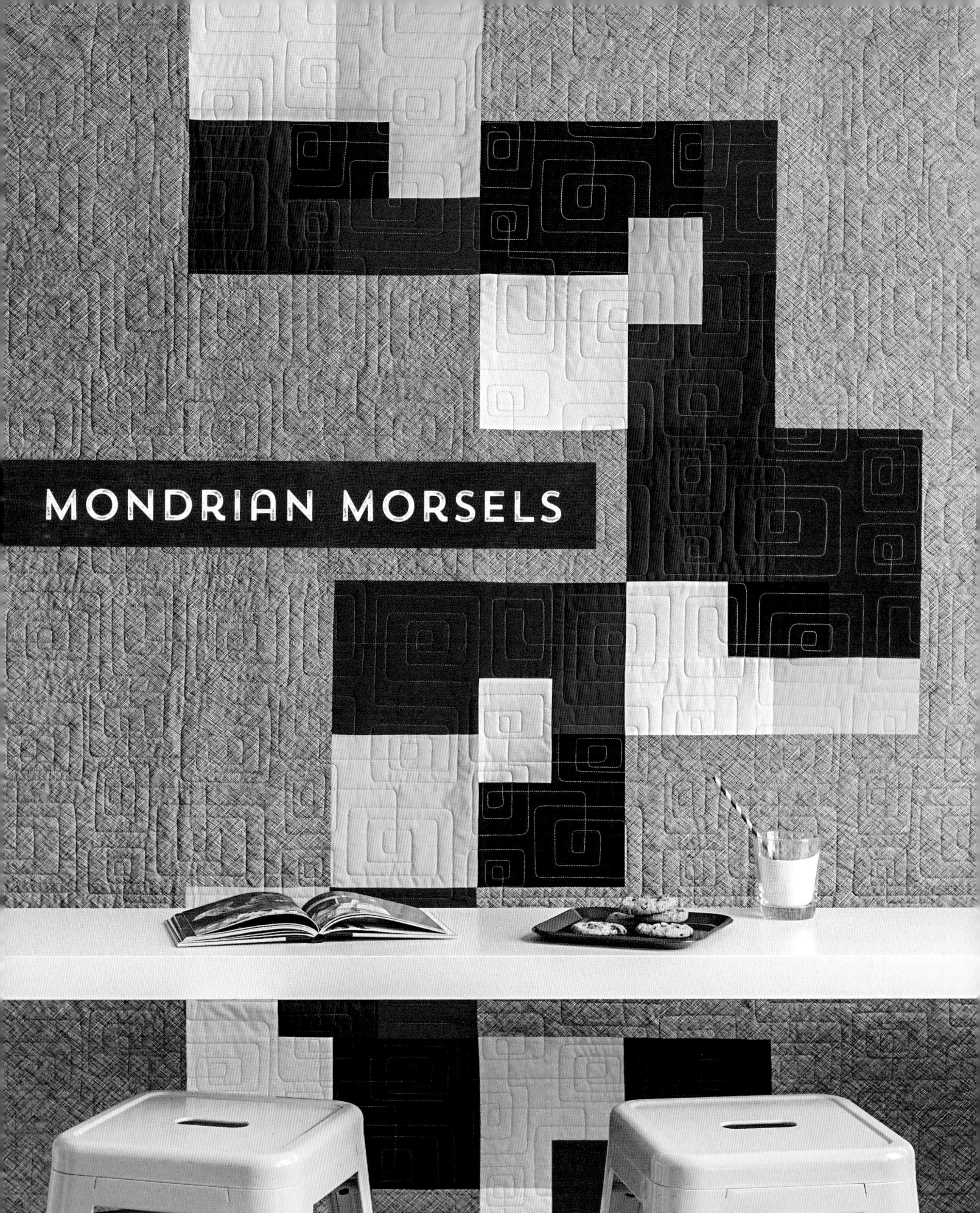

MONDRIAN MORSELS

Mondrian Morsels features the 16″ It's a Wrap block. The asymmetric staggered setting encourages twists and turns to create new shapes and focus. It's a bold statement for a big appetite! The primary color scheme of red, blue, and yellow plus black-and-white solid fabrics is reminiscent of the artist Mondrian. The textural neutral negative space adds just a little interest and allows the large-scale simple shapes to stand out. Any of the other 16″ blocks can easily be traded in this setting. Or, four 8″ blocks could replace one 16″ block to illustrate a smaller, more detailed interpretation.

A modern geometric design with rounded edges is repeated in the quilting. The neutral thread contrasts just a little with the solid colors. This quilting adds subtle texture and dimension, allowing the blocks to be the focus.

The blue binding does not compete with the design elements, yet gives the quilt an edge. It's the little detail on this plate of morsels, finishing the presentation.

Tip

It's essential to make these blocks in sets of 5, so these ingredients and instructions are for making 10 blocks. You will use 6 in the quilt top and have 4 left over. Having the extra blocks will help you make design decisions, and the remaining blocks can be used for a pillow, a runner, or in the quilt backing (see Encore Serving, page 126).

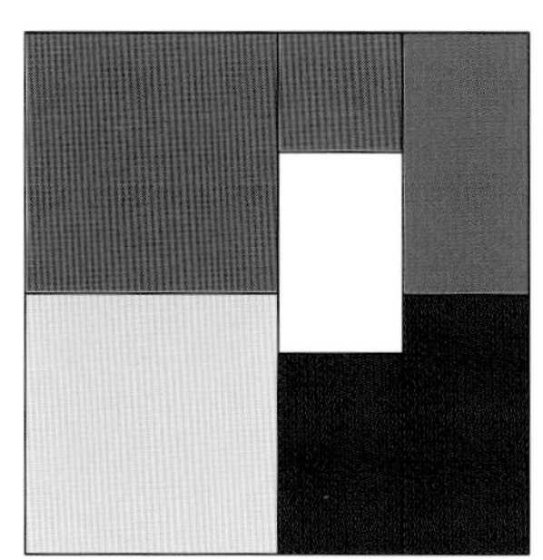

IT'S A WRAP BLOCK + STAGGERED SETTING

Finished quilt:	Finished block:	Number of blocks:
64½″ × 72½″	16″ × 16″	6

MAKE THE QUILT

Refer to the instructions for making 16″ blocks in It's a Wrap Block Recipe (page 34).

1. Make 10 blocks (2 sets of 5).

2. Referring to the quilt assembly diagram (at right), arrange the blocks and background pieces, distributing color and shapes throughout the quilt.

3. The quilt top is divided into 6 large sections, each containing a block, a short background piece, and a longer background piece. Within each section, sew the block and the short background piece together; stitch that unit to the longer background piece.

4. When you have completed all the sections, sew pairs together to make 3 horizontal rows. Sew the rows together to complete the quilt top.

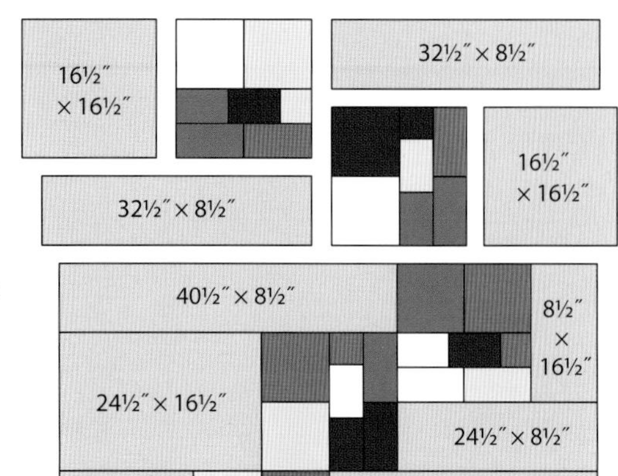

Quilt assembly

Ingredients

These yardages are based on 42″ of usable width from nondirectional fabrics.

- **5 colors:** ⅝ yard each, or 2 fat quarters each
- **Background:** 3 yards
- **Binding:** ⅝ yard (We used medium-dark blue.)
- **Quilt backing:** 73″ × 81″
- **Batting:** 73″ × 81″

Prep the Ingredients

Cut all fabrics by the width of fabric. Remove selvages before cutting.

FROM EACH COLOR:

- Cut 1 strip 17½″ × width of fabric.

  Subcut 2 squares 17½″ × 17½″.
- Refer to It's a Wrap Block Recipe, Prep the Ingredients (page 35) to stack and subcut the squares.

FOR BINDING:

- Cut 7 strips 2½″ × width of fabric.

FROM BACKGROUND:

- Cut 6 strips 8½″ × width of fabric.

  Subcut 4 strips 8½″ × 32½″.

  Subcut 1 strip 8½″ × 40½″.

  Subcut 1 strip 8½″ × 24½″.
- Cut 3 strips 16½″ × width of fabric.

  Subcut 4 squares 16½″ × 16½″.

  Subcut 1 rectangle 16½″ × 24½″.

  Subcut 1 rectangle 16½″ × 8½″.

Mondrian Morsels, 64½″ × 72½″, made by Jill Guffy, machine quilted by April West with the Geometric Path pantograph by Kristin Hoftyzer, 2014

SPRING ROLLS

*S*pring Rolls uses 8″ Sushi blocks in a radiating setting. The blocks are more densely arranged in the upper center. The diagonal lines of the Sushi block make it look as if the blocks spin off and radiate from the visually weighted center to the quilt edges. There is an appealing asymmetrical randomness to the orientation and the placement of the blocks.

A range of yellow green is common to all the fabrics. The background is white with a print of "stitches." The use of the multicolor stripe adds interest and broadens the color palette. The dark green commands attention and leads the eye all around the quilt.

Quilting lines travel in an organic pattern that was chosen not to compete with the hard-edged shapes in the block.

Spring Rolls is bound in light green, adding an edge of color to the large areas of negative space.

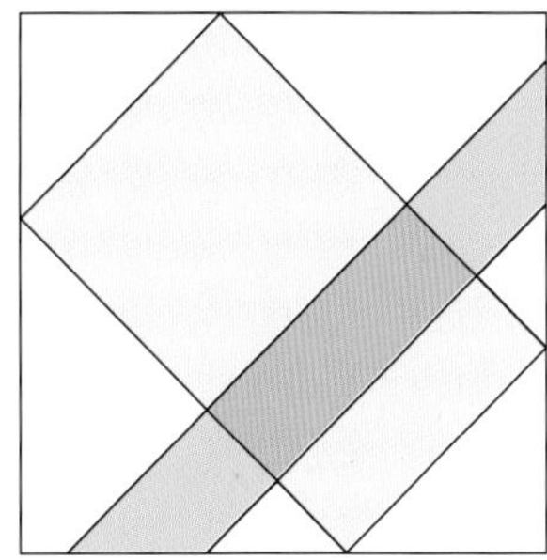

SUSHI BLOCK + RADIATING SETTING

Finished quilt:	Finished block:	Number of blocks:
48½″ × 64½″	8″ × 8″	15

Ingredients

These yardages are based on 42″ of usable width of fabric, with nondirectional fabric for the background. You can use directional fabrics for the light, medium, and dark fabrics. See Using Stripes (page 41).

- **Light (light yellow green):** ½ yard
- **Medium (stripe):** ½ yard
- **Dark (dark yellow green):** ¼ yard if nondirectional, ½ yard if directional
- **Background (cream with print):** 1 yard for blocks and 1⅞ yards for quilt setting pieces
- **Binding:** ½ yard (We used light yellow green.)
- **Quilt backing:** 57″ × 73″
- **Batting:** 57″ × 73″

Prep the Ingredients

Cut all fabrics by the width of fabric unless otherwise stated. Note that you need to cut some fabrics by the length of the fabric. Remove selvages before cutting.

FROM LIGHT:

- Cut 2 strips 6½″ × width of fabric.

  Subcut 15 rectangles 6½″ × 4¾″.

FROM MEDIUM:

- Cut 4 strips 5″ × *length* of fabric to yield 4 rectangles 5″ × 18″.

FROM DARK:

- If *nondirectional fabric*, cut 1 strip 4¾″ × width of fabric.

  Subcut 2 rectangles 4¾ × 18″.
- If *directional fabric*, cut 2 strips 4¾″ × *length* of fabric to yield 2 rectangles 4¾″ × 18″.

FOR BINDING:

- Cut 6 strips 2½″ × width of fabric.

FROM BACKGROUND:

For blocks:

- Cut 3 strips 7″ × width of fabric.

  Subcut 15 squares 7″ × 7″.

  Subcut each square once diagonally to yield 30 large triangles.
- Cut 2 strips 5″ × width of fabric.

  Subcut 15 squares 5″ × 5″.

  Subcut each square once diagonally to yield 30 small triangles.

For quilt setting pieces:

- Cut 3 strips 8½″ × width of fabric. From each strip:

  Subcut 1 rectangle 8½″ × 24½″.

  Subcut 1 rectangle 8½″ × 16½″.
- Cut 2 strips 8½″ × width of fabric. From each strip:

  Subcut 1 rectangle 8½″ × 24½″.

  Subcut 2 squares 8½″ × 8½″.
- Cut 2 strips 8½″ × width of fabric.

  From 1 strip, subcut 2 squares 8½″ × 8½″.

  Using 1 strip and the remaining partial strip, piece and subcut 1 rectangle 8½″ × 48½″.

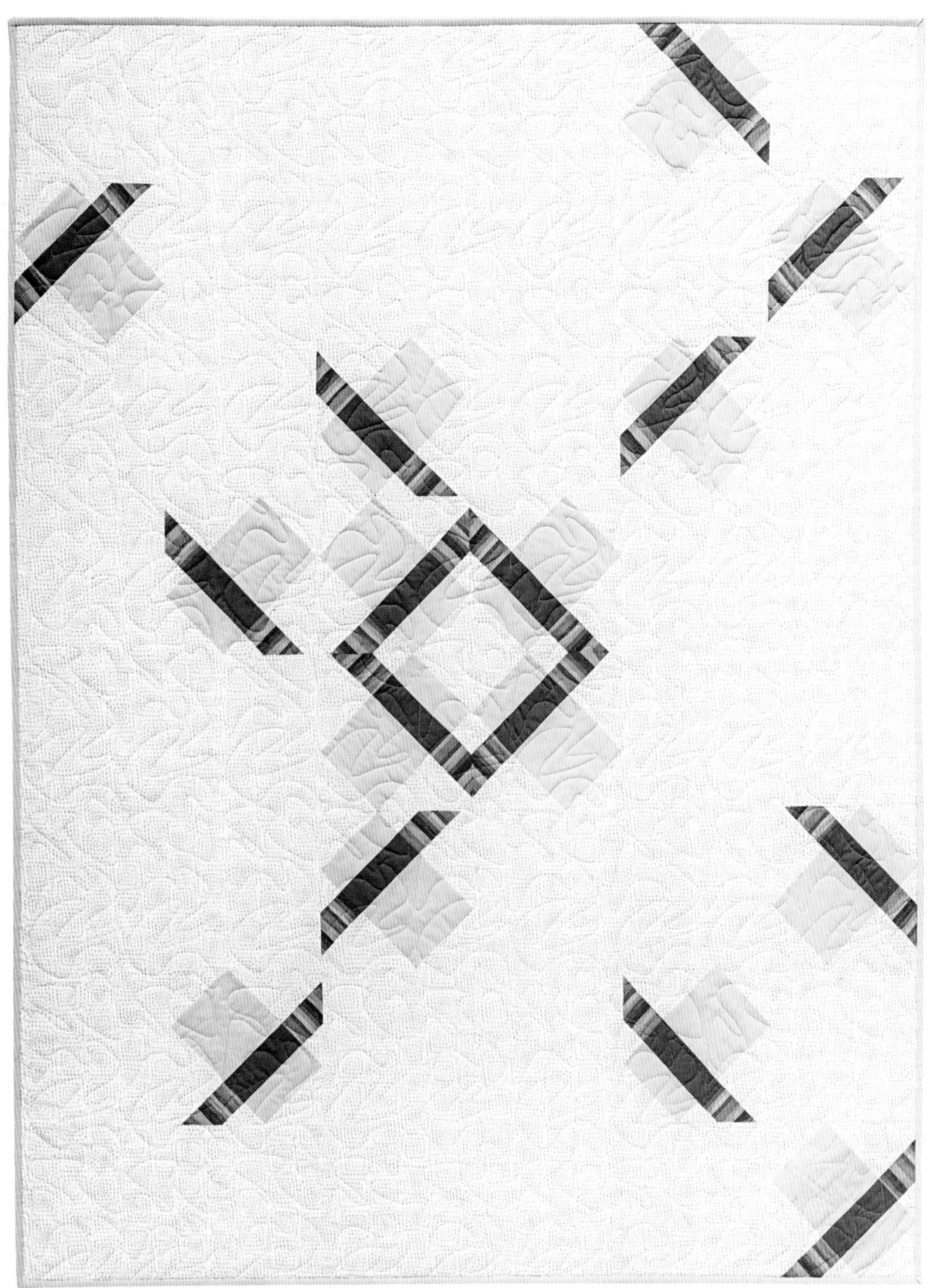

Spring Rolls, 48½″ × 64½″, made by Marny Buck, machine quilted by April West using the Sydney pantograph by Kim Darwin, 2014

MAKE THE QUILT

Refer to Sushi Block Recipe, Make the Block (page 41), for the instructions for making 8″ blocks.

1. Make 15 Sushi blocks.

2. Referring to the quilt assembly diagram, arrange and sew the blocks and background pieces in 6 columns.

3. Sew the columns together to complete the quilt top.

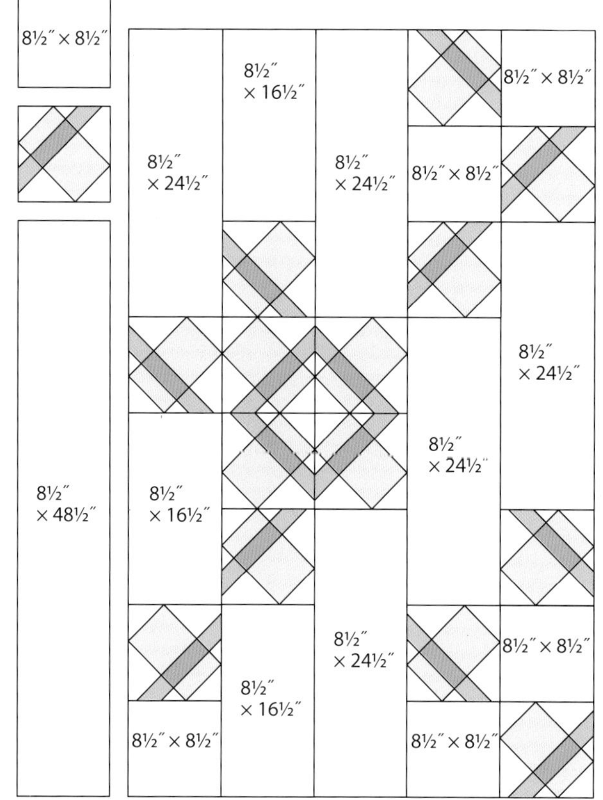

Quilt assembly

SETTINGS MENU

SIZE AND LAYOUT OPTIONS TO MAKE IT YOUR OWN

Grid Setting	70	Straight-Line Setting	80
Repeated Horizontal Setting	72	Staggered Setting	84
Diagonal-Line Setting	76	Radiating Setting	86

Think of the six quilt settings we offer as templates for setting a lovely table. A beautiful and appropriate table setting contributes to the success of a meal. All table settings include glasses, flatware, and napkins. The way they use color, formality, proportion, and shine or matte set the tone for the meal.

Similarly, a quilt layout provides the structure needed to balance positive and negative spaces, block sizes, shapes, lines, color, and value.

Captions under each of the multisized settings offer the number and size of blocks needed, nondirectional background yardage, cuts to get you started, background piece measurements, and binding information.

Choose a block, check the ingredient lists with the block instructions, and get started on your successful meal!

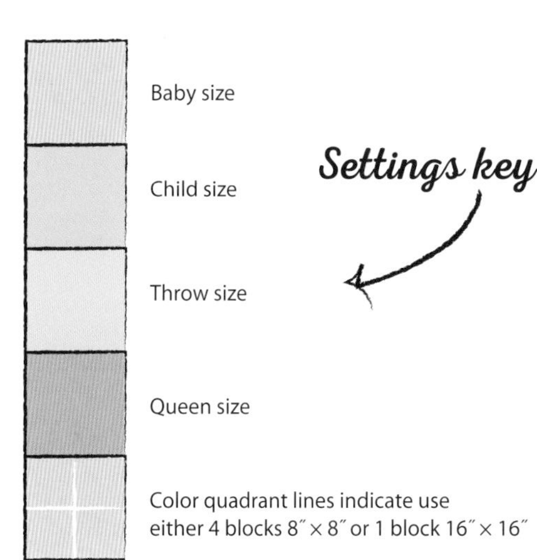

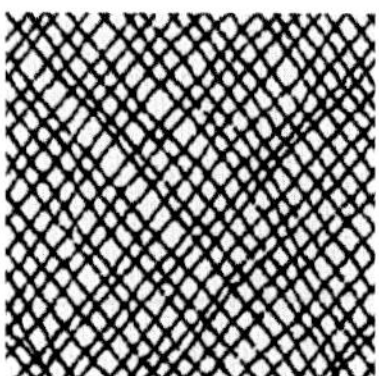

GRID SETTING

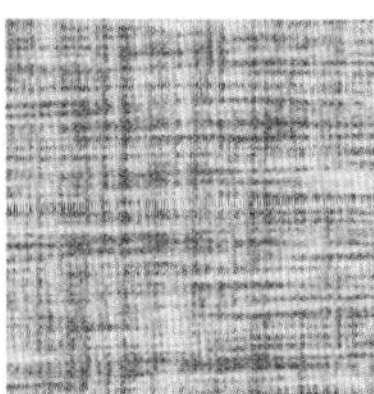
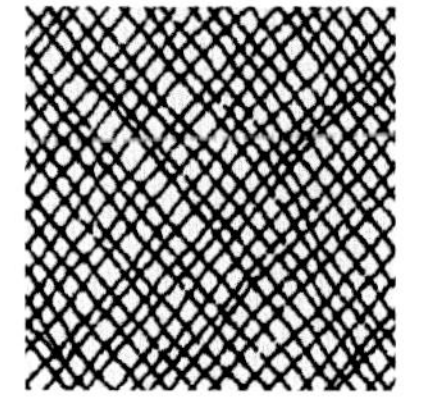

We start with the familiar grid setting, which comprises blocks evenly distributed in an allover pattern. *Antipasto Platter* (page 44) and *Éclairs* (page 102) use grid settings. In both, the blocks fill the grid. You could choose to leave some spaces in the grid open. Alternating blocks with background squares is a traditional example of this. Or you might fill columns or rows with background, symmetrically or asymmetrically. The grid offers you freedom to be your own designer!

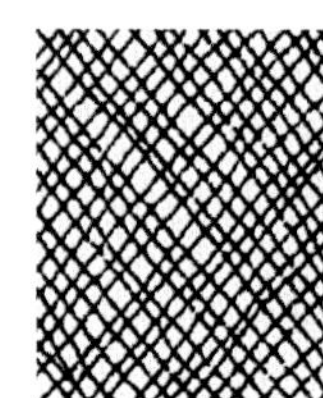

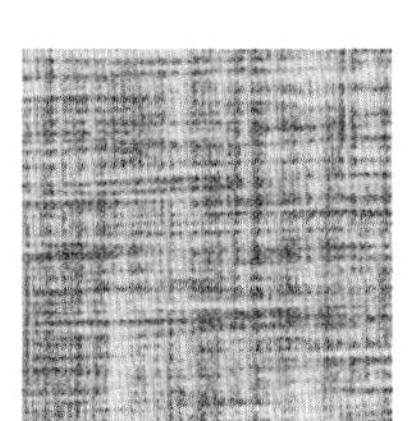

QUILT SIZE GUIDE FOR 8″ BLOCKS

- **Baby:** 40½″ × 48½″, 30 blocks, ½ yard binding (5 strips)
- **Child:** 48½″ × 64½″, 48 blocks, ½ yard binding (6 strips)
- **Throw:** 64½″ × 80½″, 80 blocks, ⅔ yard binding (8 strips)
- **Queen:** 96½″ × 96½″, 144 blocks, ⅞ yard binding (10 strips)

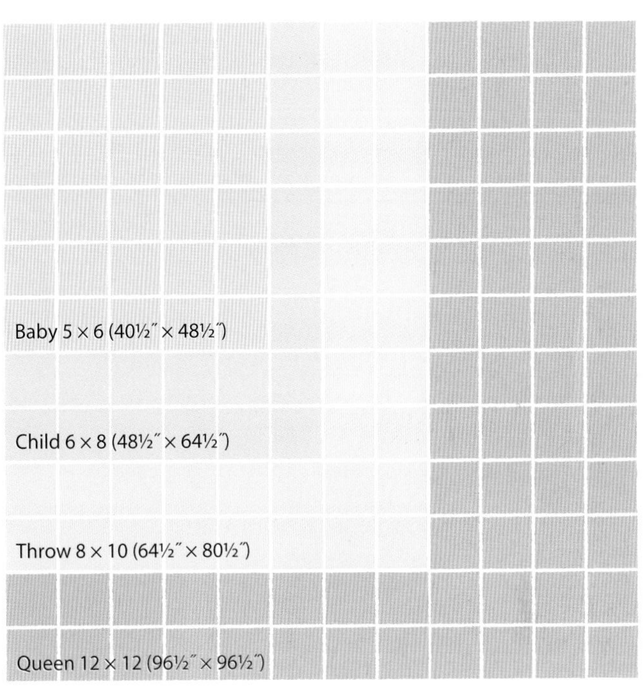

QUILT SIZE GUIDE FOR 16″ BLOCKS

- **Baby:** 48½″ × 48½″, 9 blocks, ½ yard binding (5–6 strips)
- **Child:** 48½″ × 64½″, 12 blocks, ½ yard binding (6 strips)
- **Throw:** 64½″ × 80½″, 20 blocks, ⅔ yard binding (8 strips)
- **Queen:** 96½″ × 96½″, 36 blocks, ⅞ yard binding (10 strips)

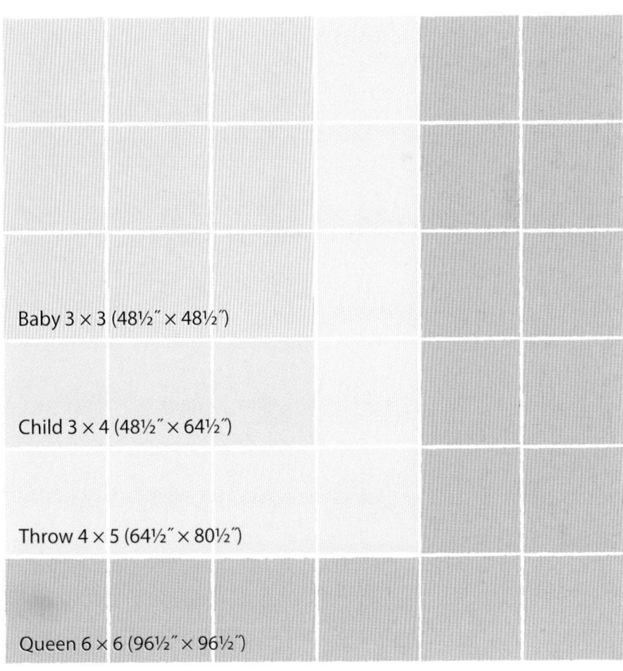

REPEATED HORIZONTAL SETTING

The repeated horizontal setting incorporates random negative space while allowing the block elements to "read" horizontally. It's an organized, calming recipe with unpredictable spacing between blocks for intrigue.

Certainly these spaces and blocks can be rearranged to suit your preference; color and value will play a role. A feature of *Snack Circuit* (page 48) is the negative space within the Salsa block (or any of the other blocks depending on their arrangement). This increased negative space can bleed into the background, creating other isolated shapes and lines. In *Petits Fours* (page 112), It's a Wrap block shapes are more defined and connected with an accent line. It is more symmetrical, predictable.

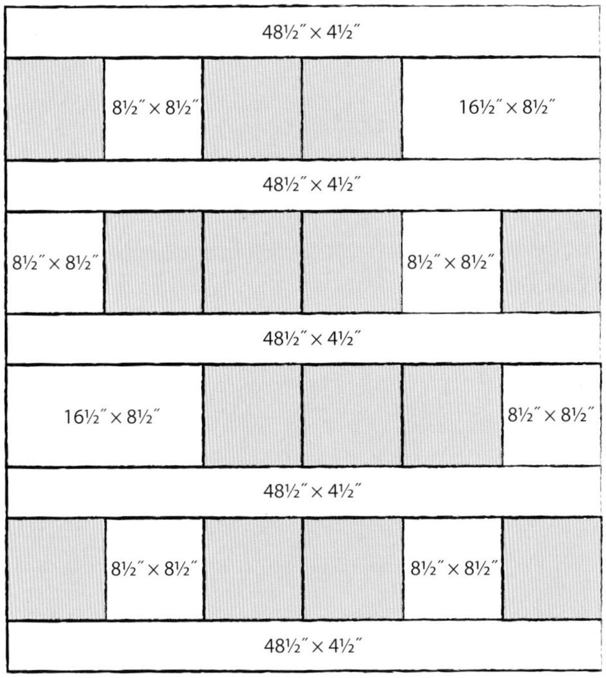

48½″ × 4½″
8½″ × 8½″ 16½″ × 8½″
48½″ × 4½″
8½″ × 8½″ 8½″ × 8½″
48½″ × 4½″
16½″ × 8½″ 8½″ × 8½″
48½″ × 4½″
8½″ × 8½″ 8½″ × 8½″
48½″ × 4½″

BABY SIZE FOR 8″ BLOCKS

- 48½″ × 52½″
- 14 blocks
- 1½ yards nondirectional background

  Subcut:

  2 strips 8½″ × width of fabric (subcut each into 1 rectangle 8½″ × 16½″ and 3 squares 8½″ × 8½″)

  5 strips 4½″ × width of fabric
- ½ yard binding (6 strips)
- Quilt backing: 57″ × 61″
- Batting: 57″ × 61″

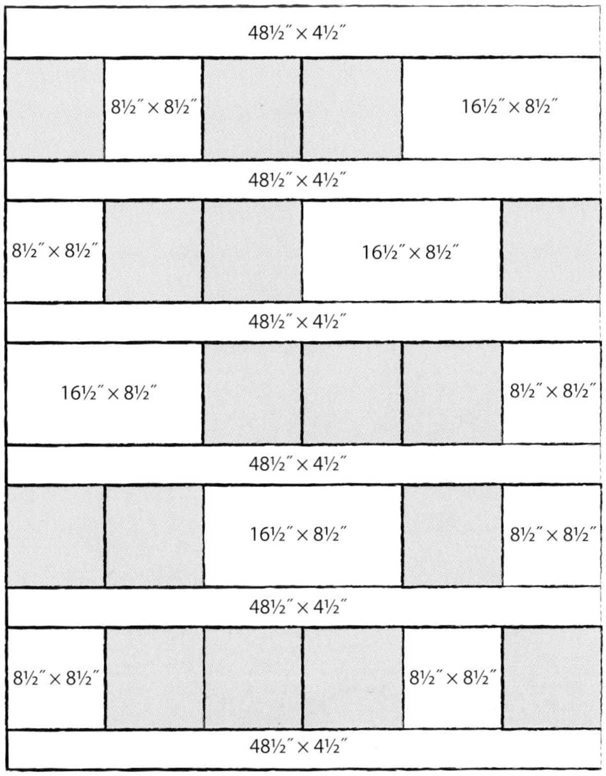

48½″ × 4½″
8½″ × 8½″ 16½″ × 8½″
48½″ × 4½″
8½″ × 8½″ 16½″ × 8½″
48½″ × 4½″
16½″ × 8½″ 8½″ × 8½″
48½″ × 4½″
16½″ × 8½″ 8½″ × 8½″
48½″ × 4½″
8½″ × 8½″ 8½″ × 8½″
48½″ × 4½″

CHILD SIZE FOR 8″ BLOCKS

- 48½″ × 64½″
- 16 blocks
- 2 yards nondirectional background (3 strips 8½″ × width of fabric and 8 strips 4½″ × width of fabric)
- ½ yard binding (6 strips)
- Quilt backing: 57″ × 73″
- Batting: 57″ × 73″

THROW SIZE FOR 8″ OR 16″ BLOCKS

- 64½″ × 72½″
- 32 blocks if 8″, 8 blocks if 16″
- 2⅜ yards nondirectional background (2 strips 16½″ × width of fabric and 7 strips 6½″ × width of fabric)
- ⅔ yard binding (8 strips)
- Quilt backing: 73″ × 81″
- Batting: 73″ × 81″

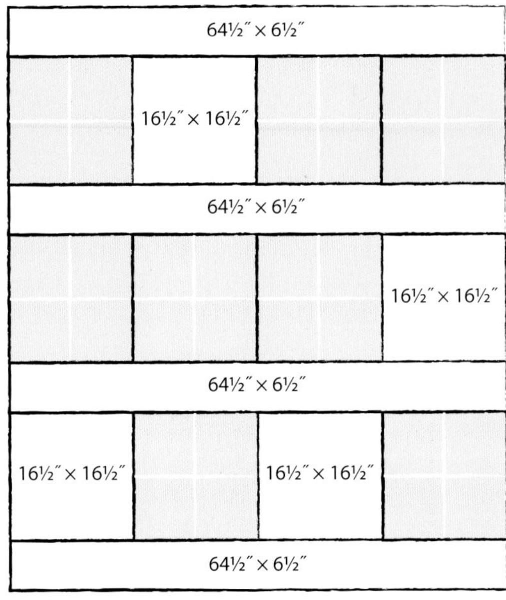

QUEEN SIZE FOR 16″ BLOCKS

- 96½″ × 94½″
- 16 blocks
- 4⅜ yards nondirectional background (4 strips 16½″ × width of fabric and 13 strips 6½ × width of fabric)
- ⅞ yard binding (10 strips)
- Quilt backing: 105″ × 103″
- Batting: 105″ × 103″

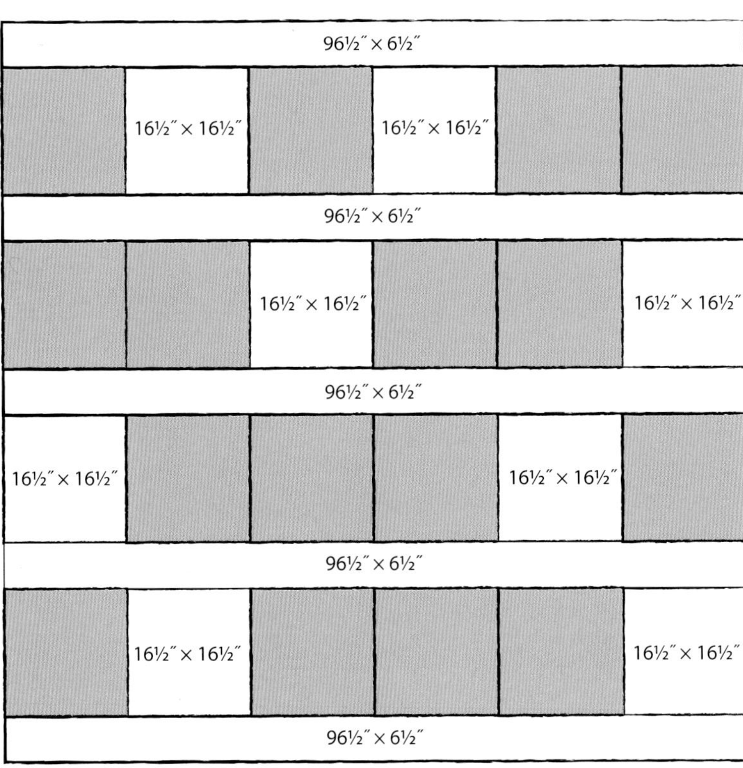

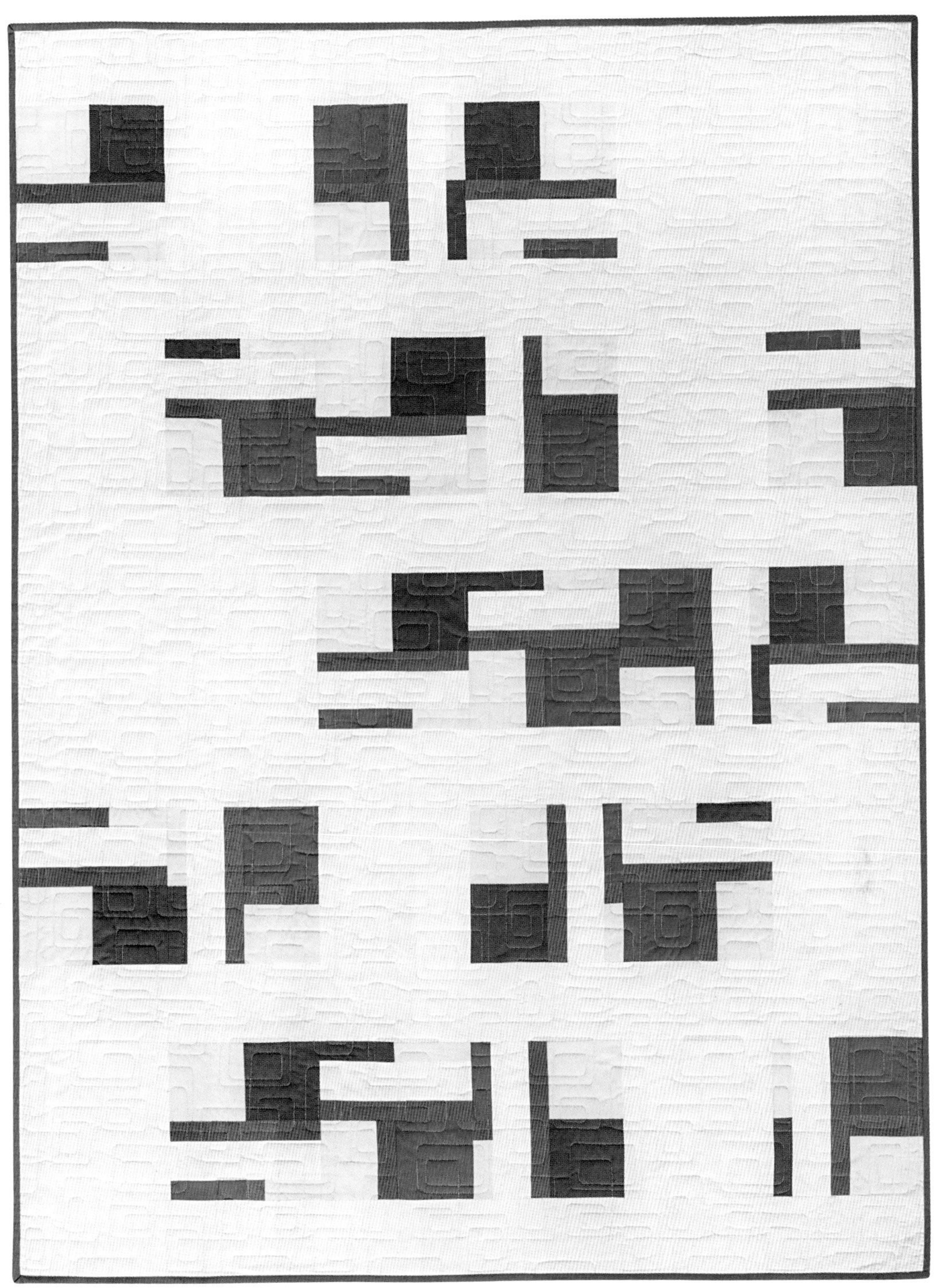

Snack Circuit (see project photo, page 51) is another variation of a repeated horizontal setting.

DIAGONAL-LINE SETTING

In the diagonal setting, blocks stream across the quilt from the upper left to the lower right. This diagonal line, balanced with negative space on either side, makes a powerful graphic statement.

Bottle Stoppers (page 52) and *Sweet Endings* (page 118) illustrate the diagonal setting. The diagrammed block placements allow for visual overlaps, groupings of four blocks side by side, and stair stepping. Different shapes and patterns will form depending on the block you choose and the way you place your blocks side by side. All the quilts are square, so you can place the diagonal line starting from either the upper left or the upper right.

8½″ × 8½″
8½″ × 16½″
8½″ × 24½″
8½″ × 24½″
8½″ × 16½″
8½″ × 8½″

BABY SIZE FOR 8″ BLOCKS

- 40½″ × 40½″
- 13 blocks
- ⅞ yard nondirectional background (3 strips 8½″ × width of fabric)
- ½ yard binding (5 strips)
- Quilt backing: 49″ × 49″
- Batting: 49″ × 49″

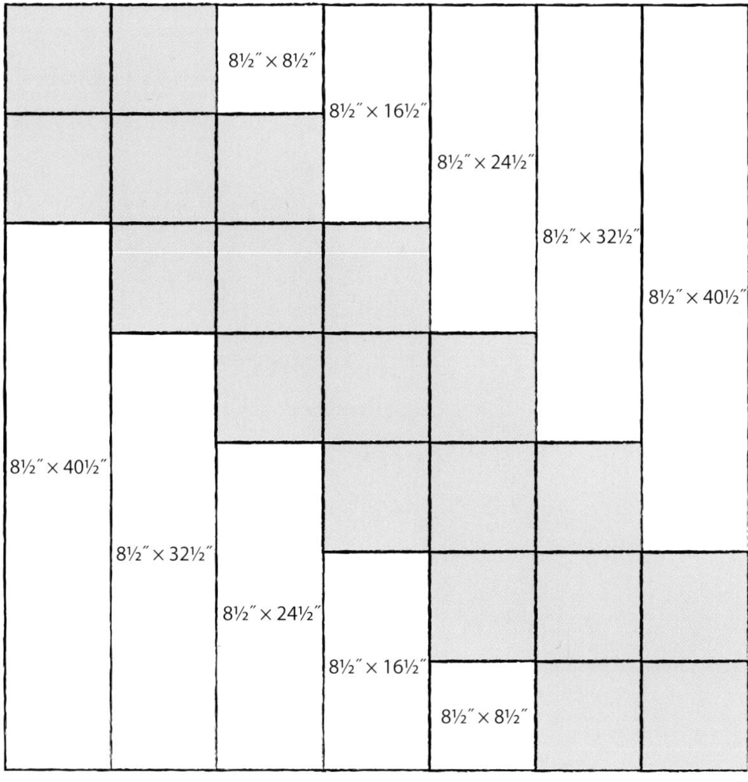

CHILD SIZE FOR 8″ BLOCKS

- 56½″ × 56½″
- 19 blocks
- 1½ yards nondirectional background (6 strips 8½″ × width of fabric)
- ½ yard binding (6 strips)
- Quilt backing: 65″ × 65″
- Batting: 65″ × 65″

8½″ × 8½″
8½″ × 16½″
8½″ × 24½″
8½″ × 32½″
8½″ × 40½″
8½″ × 48½″
8½″ × 48½″
8½″ × 40½″
8½″ × 32½″
8½″ × 24½″
8½″ × 16½″
8½″ × 8½″

THROW SIZE FOR 8″ BLOCKS

- 64½″ × 64½″
- 22 blocks
- 2¼ yards nondirectional background (9 strips 8½″ × width of fabric)
- ⅝ yard binding (7 strips)
- Quilt backing: 73″ × 73″
- Batting: 73″ × 73″

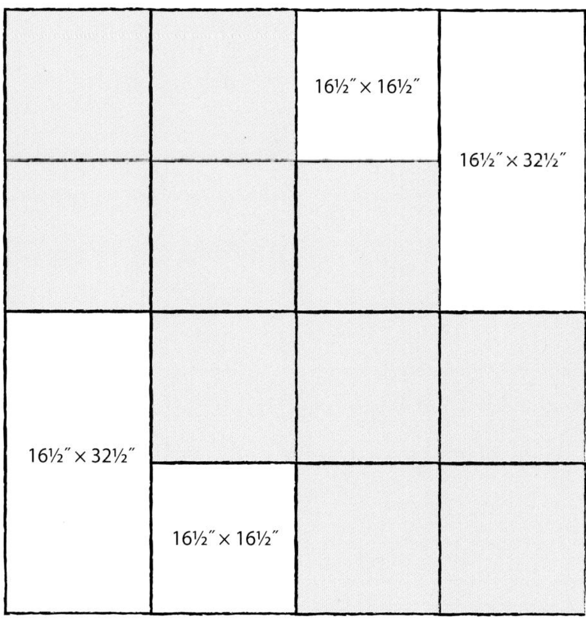

THROW SIZE FOR 16″ BLOCKS

- 64½″ × 64½″
- 10 blocks
- 1½ yards nondirectional background (3 strips 16½″ × width of fabric)
- ⅝ yard binding (7 strips)
- Quilt backing: 73″ × 73″
- Batting: 73″ × 73″

16½″ × 16½″

16½″ × 32½″

16½″ × 48½″

16½″ × 64½″

16½″ × 64½″

16½″ × 48½″

16½″ × 32½″

16½″ × 16½″

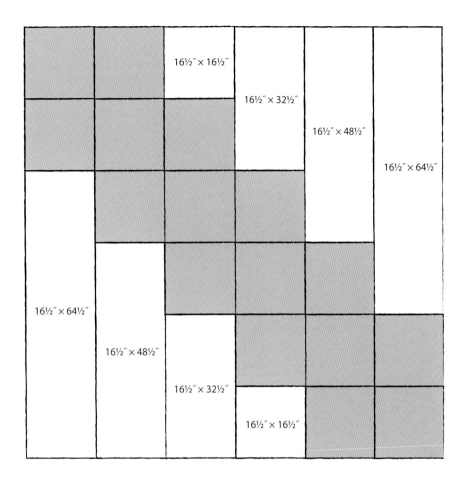

QUEEN SIZE FOR 16″ BLOCKS

- 96½″ × 96½″
- 16 blocks
- 3⅞ yards nondirectional background (8 strips 16½″ × width of fabric)
- ⅞ yard binding (10 strips)
- Quilt backing: 105″ × 105″
- Batting: 105″ × 105″

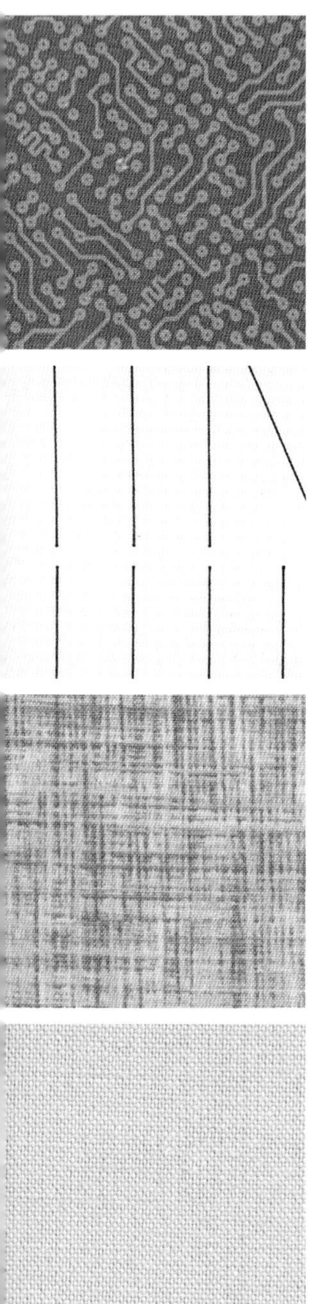

STRAIGHT-LINE SETTING

(HORIZONTAL, VERTICAL, CROSSED)

These straightforward block presentations are a minimalist approach to modern design. The horizontal setting is restful and calm. The vertical column, solidly grounded, commands a sense of dominance. The sizes of the featured blocks in the columns and rows are pleasingly proportionate to the background. Asymmetry and ample negative space allow the blocks to be the focus. *Easy as Pie* (page 96) illustrates this minimal vertical setting, using the 16″ block with just a little added strip for interest.

For each quilt size, we've chosen options based on block proportion to background. The baby size is shown with only the 8″ block. Many of the other sizes allow you to choose either block size. Using 16″ blocks creates a large-scale look; if you substitute four of the 8″ blocks for each 16″ block, you will achieve a more detailed look.

The crossed setting features small sashing lines. The blocks appear to float because these strips integrate with the background. In *Dippers* (page 56), the sashing creates a smooth continuation between the undulating rhythms of the blocks.

The baby- and the queen-size settings are square. They can be oriented either horizontally or vertically.

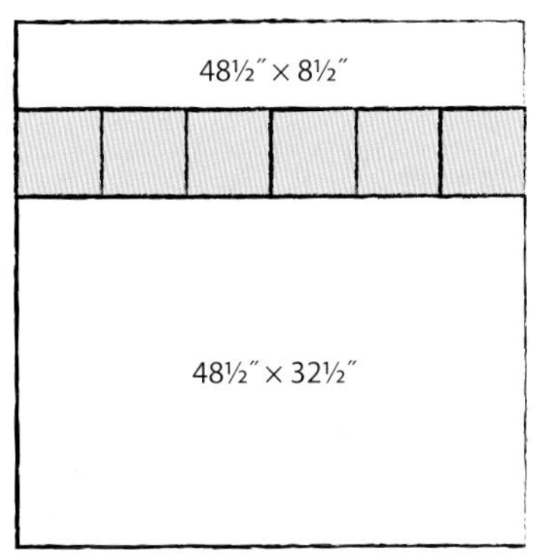

HORIZONTAL/VERTICAL

Baby Size for 8″ Blocks

- 48½″ × 48½″
- 6 blocks
- 1½ yards nondirectional background (1 strip 48½″ × width of fabric)
- ½ yard binding (5 strips)
- Quilt backing: 57″ × 57″
- Batting: 57″ × 57″

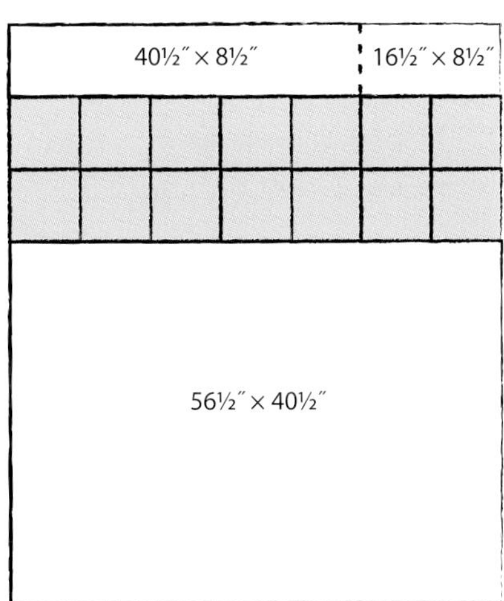

HORIZONTAL

Child Size for 8″ Blocks

- 56½″ × 64½″
- 14 blocks
- 2¼ yards nondirectional background (1 strip 56½″ × width of fabric and 2 strips 8½″ × width of fabric)
- ⅝ yard binding (7 strips)
- Quilt backing: 65″ × 73″
- Batting: 65″ × 73″

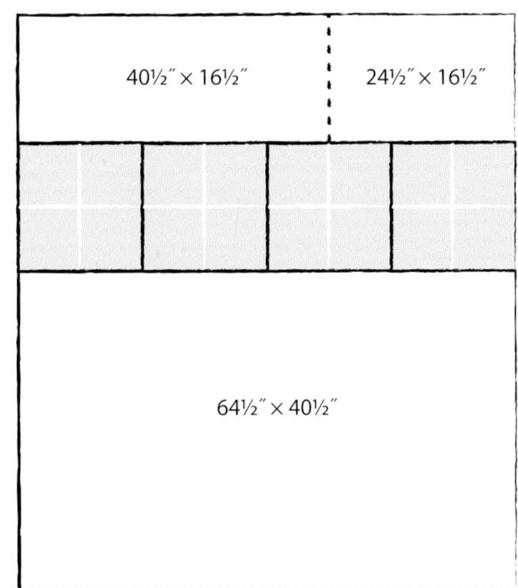

HORIZONTAL

Throw Size for 8″ or 16″ Blocks

- 64½″ × 72½″
- 16 blocks if 8″, 4 blocks if 16″
- 3 yards nondirectional background (1 strip 64½″ × width of fabric and 2 strips 16½″ × width of fabric)
- ⅔ yard binding (8 strips)
- Quilt backing: 73″ × 81″
- Batting: 73″ × 81″

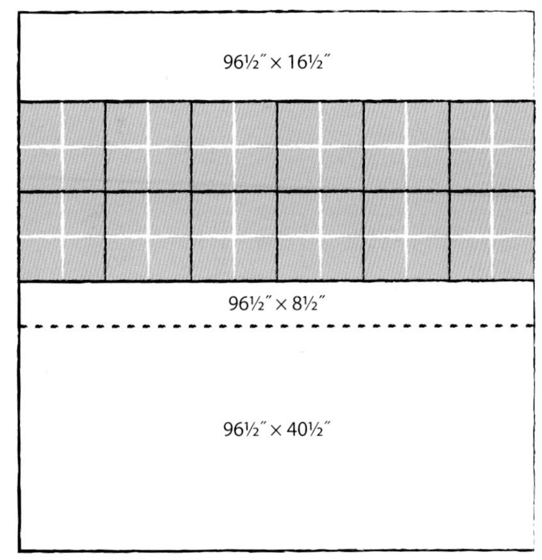

HORIZONTAL/VERTICAL

Queen Size for 8″ or 16″ Blocks

- 96½″ × 96½″
- 48 blocks if 8″, 12 blocks if 16″
- 5⅝ yards nondirectional background (2 strips 96½″ × width of fabric)
- ⅞ yard binding (10 strips)
- Quilt backing: 105″ × 105″
- Batting: 105″ × 105″

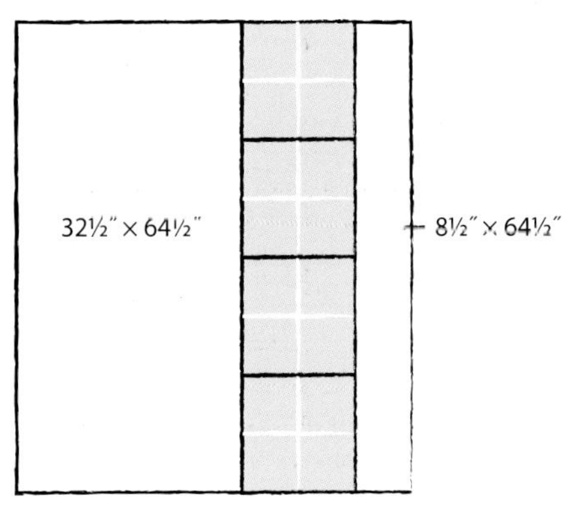

VERTICAL

Child Size for 8″ or 16″ Blocks

- 56½″ × 64½″
- 16 blocks if 8″, 4 blocks if 16″
- 2 yards nondirectional background (1 strip 64½″ × width of fabric)
- ⅝ yard binding (7 strips)
- Quilt backing: 65″ × 73″
- Batting: 65″ × 73″

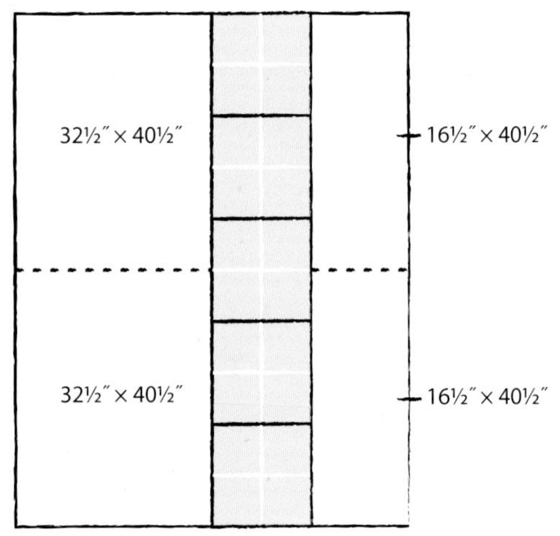

VERTICAL

Throw Size for 8″ or 16″ Blocks

- 64½″ × 80½″
- 20 blocks if 8″, 5 blocks if 16″
- 2⅞ yards nondirectional background (2 strips 32½″ × width of fabric and 2 strips 16½″ × width of fabric)
- ⅔ yard binding (8 strips)
- Quilt backing: 73″ × 89″
- Batting: 73″ × 89″

CROSSED

Baby Size for 8″ Blocks

- 46½″ × 46½″
- 9 blocks
- 1½ yards nondirectional sashing and background (sashing: 1 strip 8½″ × width of fabric; background: 1 strip 28½″ × width of fabric and 1 strip 10½″ × width of fabric)
- ½ yard binding (5 strips)
- Quilt backing: 55″ × 55″
- Batting: 55″ × 55″

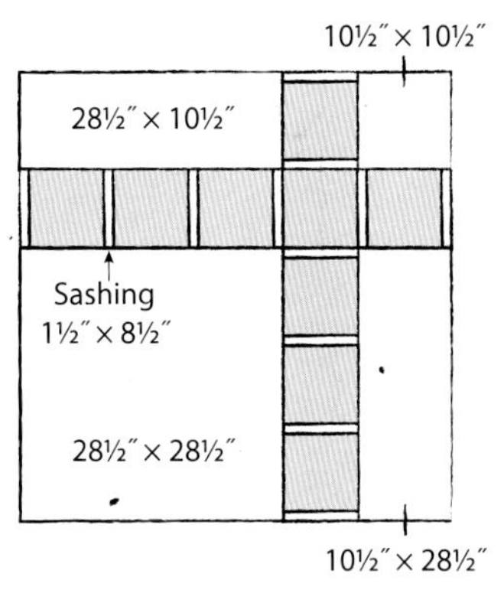

CROSSED

Throw Size for 8″ Blocks

- 55½″ × 73½″
- 13 blocks
- 3¼ yards nondirectional sashing and background, (sashing: 1 strip 8½″ × width of fabric; background: 2 strips 28½″ × width of fabric and 2 strips 19½″ × width of fabric)
- ⅝ yard binding (7 strips)
- Quilt backing: 64″ × 82″
- Batting: 64″ × 82″

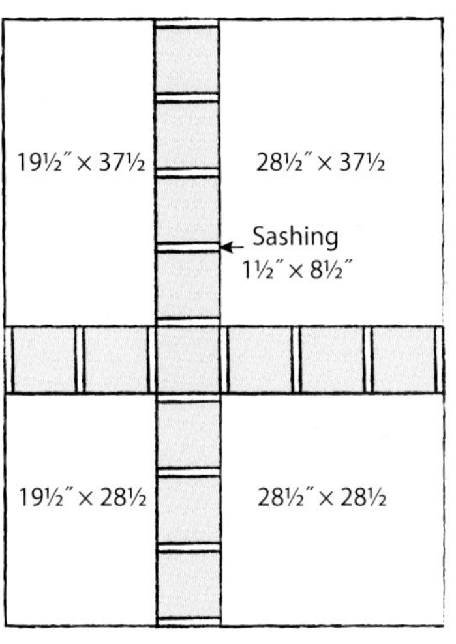

CROSSED

Queen Size for 16″ Blocks

- 92½″ × 92½″
- 9 blocks
- 5 yards nondirectional sashing and background (sashing: 1 strip 16½″ × width of fabric; background: 2 strips 20½″ × width of fabric and 2 strips 56½″ × width of fabric)
- ⅞ yard binding (10 strips)
- Quilt backing: 101″ × 101″
- Batting: 101″ × 101″

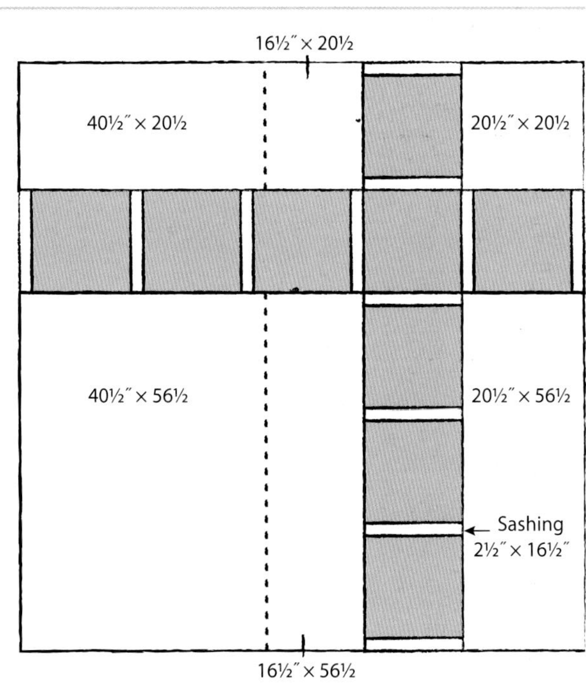

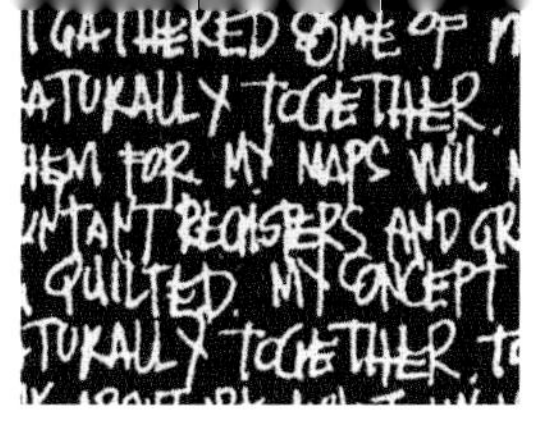

STAGGERED SETTING

Block placement in the staggered setting creates asymmetrical diagonal movement. The abundance of negative space, carried all the way to the edges of the quilt, speaks modern.

This setting offers many options: blocks, block sizes, combinations of sizes, and negative space within and outside the blocks! The *Mondrian Morsels* quilt (page 60) is a very large graphic display of rectangles and squares. The edges of the design are clearly defined with solid, saturated colors. The large-scale pyramid shape in *Glycemic Index* (page 106) floats within the negative space. The addition of the smaller blocks gives the design a sense of depth.

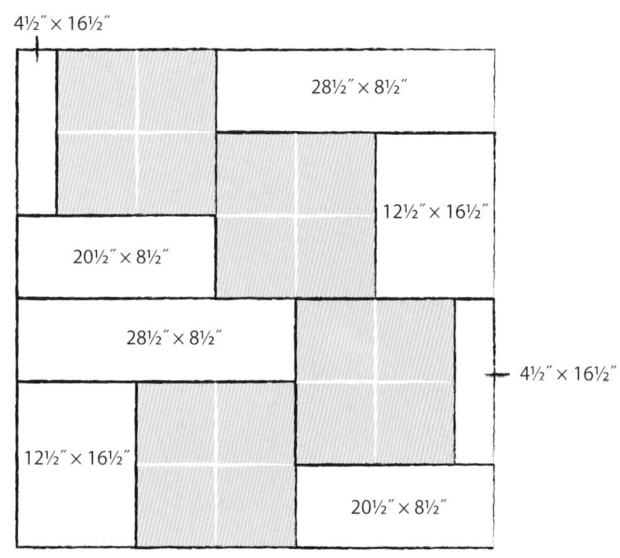

BABY SIZE FOR 8″ OR 16″ BLOCKS

- 48½″ × 48½″
- 16 blocks if 8″, 4 blocks if 16″
- 1⅜ yards nondirectional background (1 strip 16½″ × width of fabric and 3 strips 8½″ × width of fabric)
- ½ yard binding (5 strips)
- Quilt backing: 57″ × 57″
- Batting: 57″ × 57″

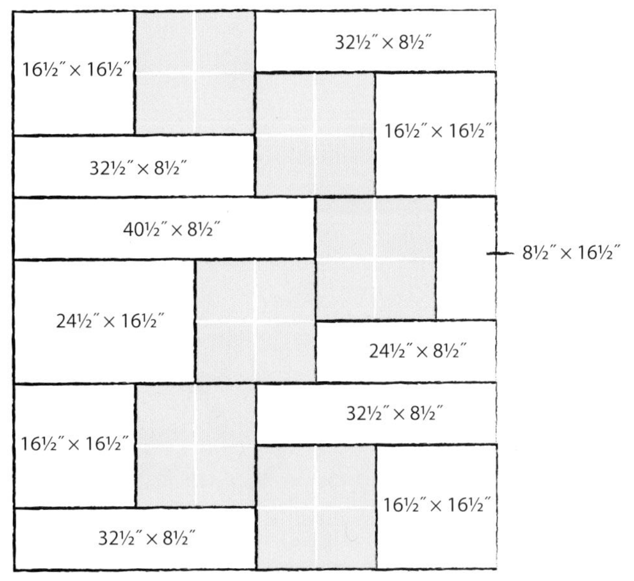

THROW SIZE FOR 8″ OR 16″ BLOCKS

- 64½″ × 72½″
- 24 blocks if 8″, 6 blocks if 16″
- 3 yards nondirectional background (3 strips 16½″ × width of fabric and 6 strips 8½″ × width of fabric)
- ⅔ yard binding (8 strips)
- Quilt backing: 73″ × 81″
- Batting: 73″ × 81″

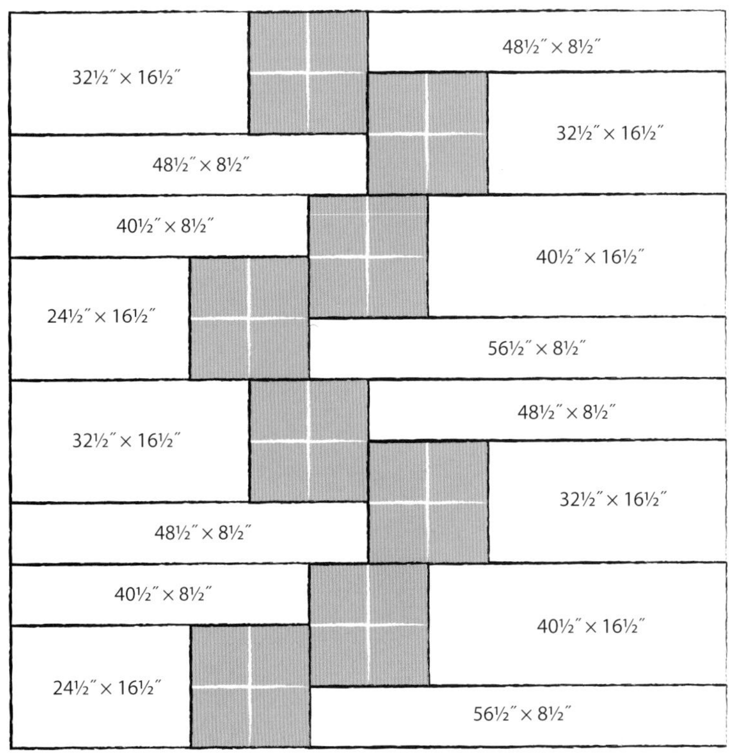

QUEEN SIZE FOR 8″ OR 16″ BLOCKS

- 96½″ × 96½″
- 32 blocks if 8″, 8 blocks if 16″
- 6¼ yards nondirectional background (8 strips 16½″ × width of fabric and 10 strips 8½″ × width of fabric)
- ⅞ yard binding (10 strips)
- Quilt backing: 105″ × 105″
- Batting: 105″ × 105″

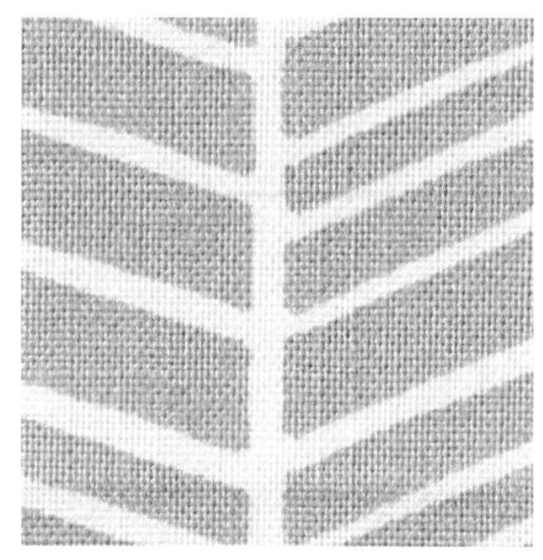

RADIATING SETTING

Blocks in this setting appear to radiate from an area of visual weight. Arranging blocks more densely in one area creates focus.

Spring Rolls (page 64) and *Tempting Turnovers* (page 90) use the radiating setting very effectively. To achieve balance in this setting, distribute color, textures, value, and shapes evenly. The large proportion of negative space working its way around the blocks supports this balance and makes a modern statement.

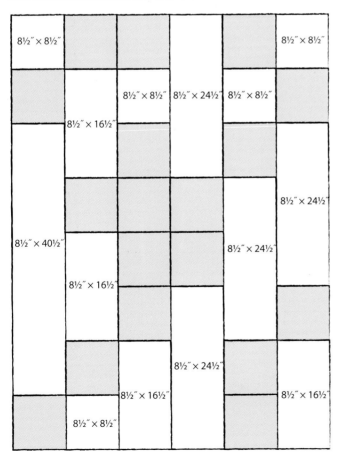

BABY SIZE FOR 8″ BLOCKS

- 48½″ × 48½″
- 13 blocks
- 1⅜ yards nondirectional background (5 strips 8½″ × width of fabric)
- ½ yard binding (5 strips)
- Quilt backing: 57″ × 57″
- Batting: 57″ × 57″

CHILD SIZE FOR 8″ BLOCKS

- 48½″ × 64½″
- 18 blocks
- 1⅞ yards nondirectional background (7 strips 8½″ × width of fabric)
- ½ yard binding (6 strips)
- Quilt backing: 57″ × 73″
- Batting: 57″ × 73″

THROW SIZE FOR 8″ OR 16″ BLOCKS

- 64½″ × 80½″
- 40 blocks if 8″, 10 blocks if 16″
- 2½ yards nondirectional background (5 strips 16½″ × width of fabric)
- ⅔ yard binding (8 strips)
- Quilt backing: 73″ × 89″
- Batting: 73″ × 89″

16½″ × 16½″
16½″ × 16½″
16½″ × 48½″
16½″ × 32½″
16½″ × 32½″
16½″ × 16½″

QUEEN SIZE FOR 8″ OR 16″ BLOCKS

- 96½″ × 96½″
- 52 blocks if 8″, 13 blocks if 16″
- 4⅝ yards nondirectional background (9 strips 16½″ × width of fabric)
- ⅞ yard binding (10 strips)
- Quilt backing: 105″ × 105″
- Batting: 105″ × 105″

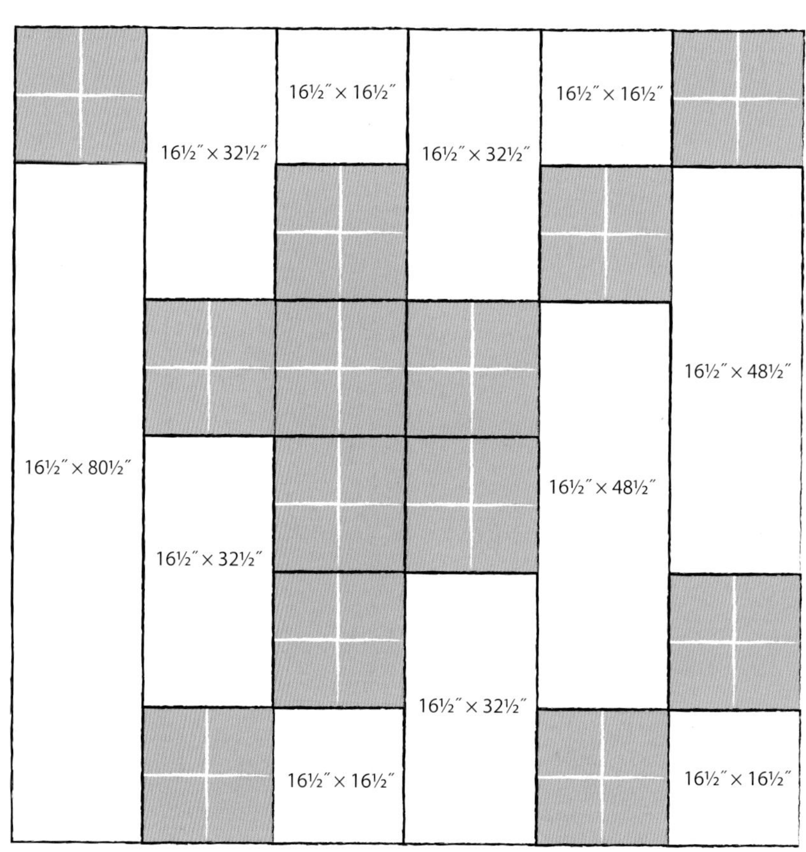

DESSERT MENU

TASTY ALTERNATIVE PROJECTS

***Tempting Turnovers* 90**
Crudités block • radiating setting

***Easy as Pie* 96**
Salsa block • vertical straight-line setting

***Éclairs* 102**
Crispy Wonton block • grid setting

***Glycemic Index* 106**
Celery Sticks block • staggered setting

***Petits Fours* 112**
It's a Wrap block • repeated horizontal setting

***Sweet Endings* 118**
Sushi block • diagonal setting

Time for the sweet course we all love, offered at the end of a fabulous meal! This menu features six irresistible quilts. See alternative settings and fresh fabrics for each of the blocks. Enjoy every bite; there won't be any calories to count.

Create the delicious Éclairs quilt from the Crispy Wonton block and grid setting.

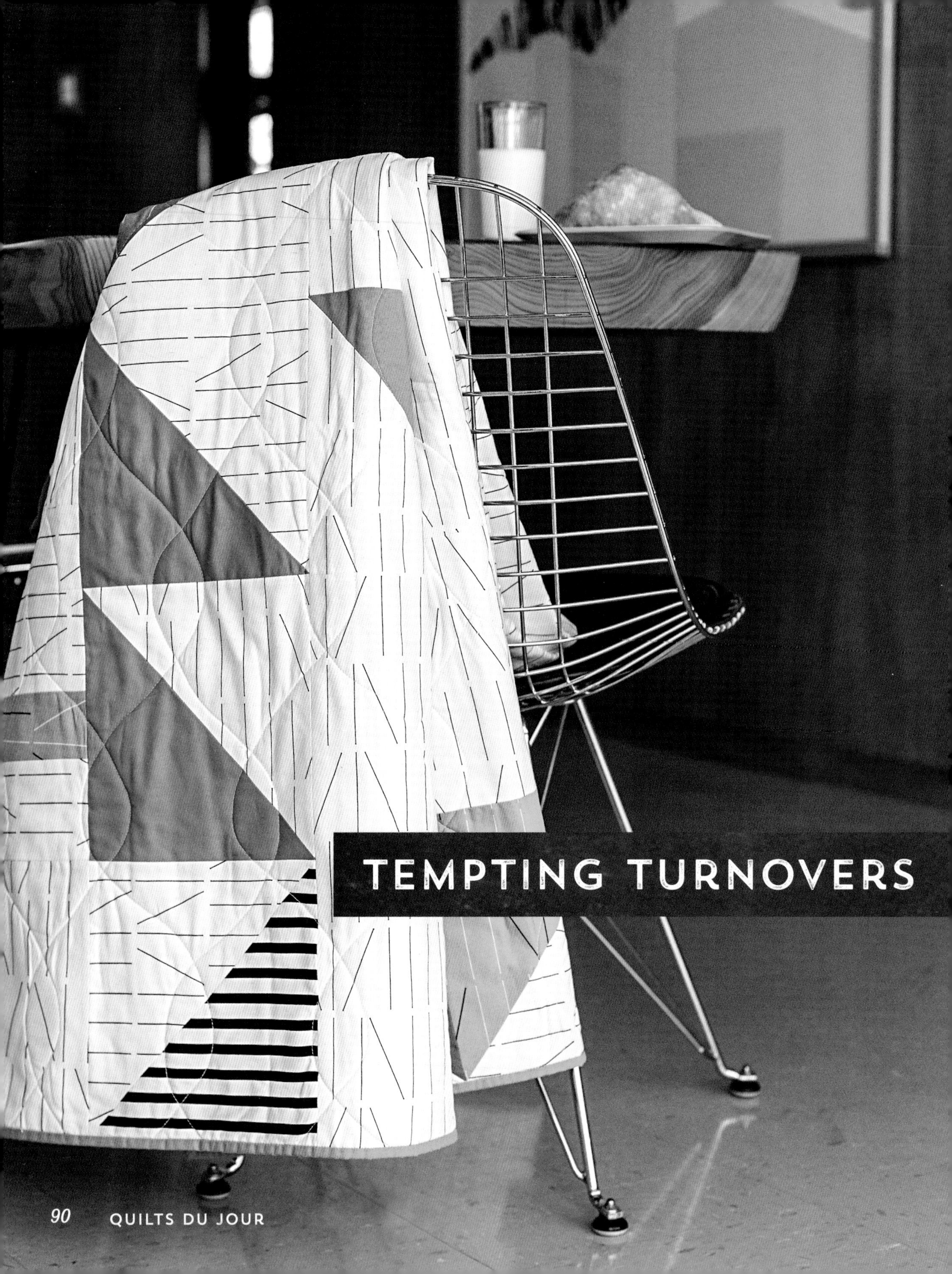

TEMPTING TURNOVERS

Tempting Turnovers places 16″ Crudités blocks in a radiating setting. The blocks are spaced more densely toward the upper left center and less densely as they radiate outward. Both the block and the setting have a large proportion of negative space, so the sense of radiating is subtle. Interplay between negative and positive shapes enlivens the quilt.

Bold, high-contrast black-and-white stripes add energy to the calmer greens, blue green, and taupes. The black lines of the background print are directional, but the print still reads as an open background because of the generous spacing between these lines. Alternating the orientation of the big background squares throughout the quilt keeps the mix of directionality balanced.

The simple curved quilting lines intersect, creating tessellating shapes across the quilt.

The solid green binding strengthens the green within the quilt and provides an edge. The small segment of black-and-white stripe in the binding offers a taste of the unexpected.

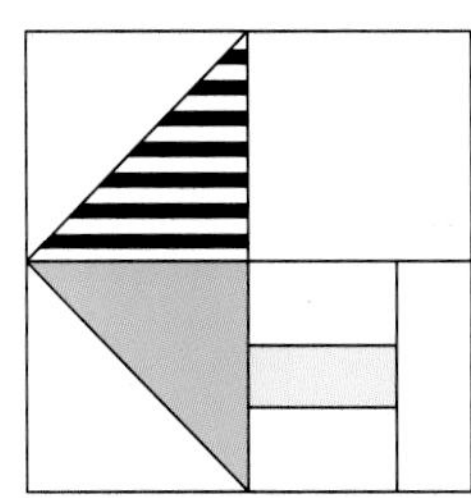

CRUDITÉS BLOCK + RADIATING SETTING

Finished quilt:	Finished block:	Number of blocks:
64½″ × 80½″	16″ × 16″	10

Ingredients

- **6 colors:** ⅓ yard each, or scraps large enough for cuts
- **Background:** 4⅝ yards
- **Binding:** ⅔ yard
- **Quilt backing:** 73″ × 89″
- **Batting:** 73″ × 89″

These yardages are based on 42″ of usable width of fabric. You can choose directional fabrics as a design choice; fabrics will be set against one another in opposing directions.

Prep the Ingredients

Cut all fabrics by the width of fabric unless otherwise stated. Remove selvages before cutting.

FROM BLUE GREEN:

- Cut 1 strip 9¼″ × width of fabric.

  Subcut 3 squares 9¼″ × 9¼″.

  Subcut 2 rectangles 2½″ × 6″.

FROM SOLID GREEN:

- Cut 1 strip 9¼″ × width of fabric.

  Subcut 2 squares 9¼″ × 9¼″.

  Subcut 2 rectangles 2½″ × 6″.

FROM LIGHTER GREEN WITH LINES:

- Cut 1 strip 9¼″ × width of fabric.

  Subcut 1 square 9¼″ × 9¼″.

  Subcut 1 rectangle 2½″ × 6″.

FROM TAUPE WITH LINES:

- Cut 1 strip 9¼″ × width of fabric.

  Subcut 1 square 9¼″ × 9¼″.

FROM SOLID TAUPE:

- Cut 1 strip 9¼″ × width of fabric.

  Subcut 2 squares 9¼″ × 9¼″.

  Subcut 2 rectangles 2½″ × 6″.

FROM BLACK-AND-WHITE STRIPE:

- Cut 1 strip 9¼″ × width of fabric.

  Subcut 2 squares 9¼″ × 9¼″.

  Subcut 4 rectangles 2½″ × 6″ (1 for binding).

FROM BACKGROUND:

For blocks:

- Cut 3 strips 9¼″ × width of fabric.

  Subcut 11 squares 9¼″ × 9¼″.

- Cut 4 strips 8½″ × width of fabric.

  Subcut 10 squares 8½″ × 8½″.

  Subcut 10 rectangles 3″ × 8½″.

- Cut 3 strips 3½″ × width of fabric.

  Subcut 20 rectangles 3½″ × 6″.

For setting squares:

- Cut 5 strips 16½″ × width of fabric.

  Subcut 10 squares 16½″ × 16½″.

FOR BINDING:

- Cut 8 strips 2½″ × width of fabric.

Tempting Turnovers, 64½″ × 80½″, made by Marny Buck, machine quilted by April West with a modified version of the Streamers pantograph by Norma Woods Sharp, 2014

Detail of *Tempting Turnovers*
(See project photo, page 93.)

MAKE THE QUILT

Refer to Crudités Block Recipe, Make the Block (page 15), for the instructions for making 16″ blocks.

1. Referring to Crudités, Make the Block, Step 1, pair the 9¼″ color squares with 9¼″ background squares to make half-square triangles.

2. Matching long sides, sew a 3½″ × 6″ background rectangle to either side of each 2½″ × 6″ color rectangle.

3. Sew a 3″ × 8½″ background rectangle to a pieced end of each unit to complete the 8½″ square bar units.

4. Using the quilt assembly diagram as a guide, arrange the half-square triangles, bar units, and 8½″ background squares into 10 scrappy blocks. There will be 2 extra half-square triangles.

Detail of *Tempting Turnovers* (see project photo, page 93). To add a bit of interest, we put a few inches of the bold striped fabric in our light green binding.

5. Sew each set of block components together to make 10 blocks 16½″ × 16½″.

6. Piece the blocks and background squares into columns.

7. Sew the columns together to complete the quilt top.

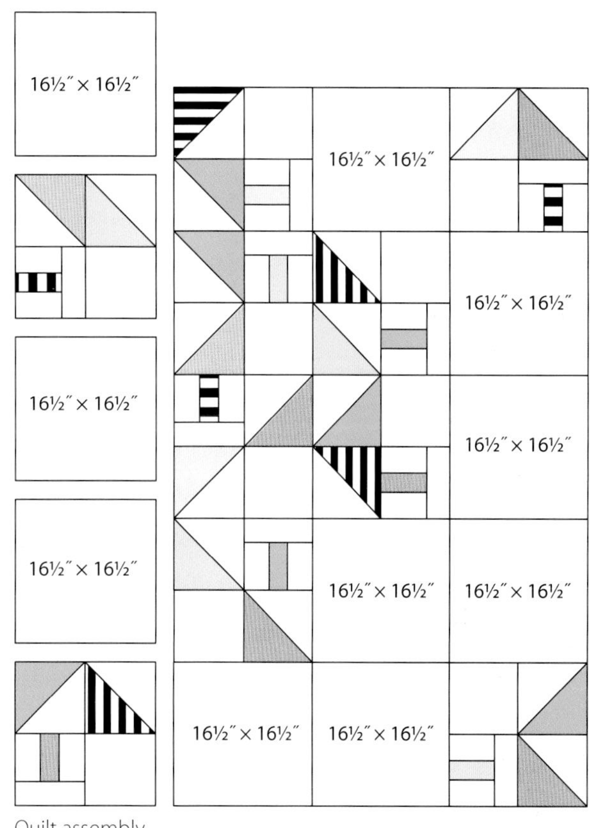

Quilt assembly

EASY AS PIE

E*asy as Pie*—this quilt is just that! Inspired by a graphic floral fat quarter bundle from the Brigitte collection by Michele D'Amore for Benartex, the large-scale Salsa blocks stack in a simplified vertical setting. The adjacent skinny line adds one more crust next to the feature. It really is all about the fabric. Less is more.

In this variation of the Salsa block, we use the background fabric in the block. The white strip bleeds into the rest of the quilt background, giving the appearance of rectangular blocks separated by sashing.

All the negative space is a perfect backdrop to feature the graphic fabrics. The overall floral quilting design mimics the motif in the fabric. Pink thread adds that necessary contrast and color to the cream background.

We used the remaining fat quarters from the collection in a scrappy binding that keeps the quilt fun.

SALSA BLOCK + VERTICAL STRAIGHT-LINE SETTING

Finished quilt:	Finished block:	Number of blocks:
64½″ × 80½″	16″ × 16″	5

Ingredients

- **Colors:** 5 fat quarters or ⅓ yard cuts of 5 fabrics (Choose some contrast between patterns with 1 near-solid as the accent fabric.)
- **Background:** ½ yard for blocks and 2¾ yards for quilt setting pieces
- **Binding:** ⅔ yard of 1 fabric or 4 fat quarters for a scrappy look
- **Quilt backing:** 73″ × 89″
- **Batting:** 73″ × 89″

Prep the Ingredients

Refer to the Salsa Block Recipe instructions (page 20).

FROM EACH FABRIC 1, 2, AND 3:

- Cut 2 strips 8½″ × 21″.

FROM FABRIC 4:

- Cut 2 strips 6½″ × 21″.

FROM ACCENT:

- Cut 7 strips 2½″ × 21″.

FOR BINDING:

- Cut 8 strips 2½″ × width of fabric.

Or, from fat quarters:

- Cut 16 strips 2½″ × 21″.

FROM BACKGROUND:

For blocks:

- Cut 3 strips 4½″ × width of fabric.

  Subcut 6 strips 4½″ × 21″ for strip sets.

For quilt setting pieces:

- Cut 2 strips 36½″ × width of fabric.
- Cut 2 strips 8½″ × width of fabric.
- Cut 2 strips 2½″ × width of fabric.

  Subcut each of these quilt setting strips to 40½″.

Easy as Pie, 64½″ × 80½″, made by Jill Guffy, machine quilted by April West using the Wall Flower pantograph by Hermione Agee, 2014

Detail of *Easy as Pie*
(See project photo, page 99.)

MAKE THE QUILT

Refer to Salsa Block Recipe, Make the Block (page 20), for the instructions for making 16″ blocks.

1. Use fabrics 1 and 2 to make 2 Step 1 strip sets. Cut into 3 segments at 8½″ intervals (2 for Block A, 1 for Block B) and 4 segments at 2½″ intervals (2 for Block C and 2 for the pieced line).

2. Use fabrics 3 and 4 and the accent fabric to make 2 Step 3 strip sets. Cut into 2 segments at 8½″ intervals (for Block C) and 6 segments at 2½″ intervals (2 for Block A, 1 for Block B, and 3 for the pieced line).

3. Use the accent fabric and block background strips to make 5 Step 5 strip sets. Cut each into 16½″ × 6½″ rectangles for Blocks A, B, and C.

4. Make the blocks: 2 A, 1 B, and 2 C.

5. Referring to the quilt assembly diagram (page 101), arrange blocks into A, C, B, C, A order. Sew together to make a 16½″ × 80½″ column.

6. Arrange the narrow strip set segments in 2, 1, 2, 1, 2 order. Sew together to make a 2½″ × 80½″ column.

Detail of *Easy as Pie* (see project photo, page 99). We used leftovers from the color fat quarters to piece this binding.

7. Sew the 2½″ × 40½″ background strips together to make a column 2½″ × 80½″.

8. Sew the 8½″ × 40½″ background strips together to make a column 8½″ × 80½″.

9. Sew the 36½″ × 40½″ background rectangles together to make a column 36½″ × 80½″.

10. Sew background columns together with the block and narrow strip columns to complete the quilt top.

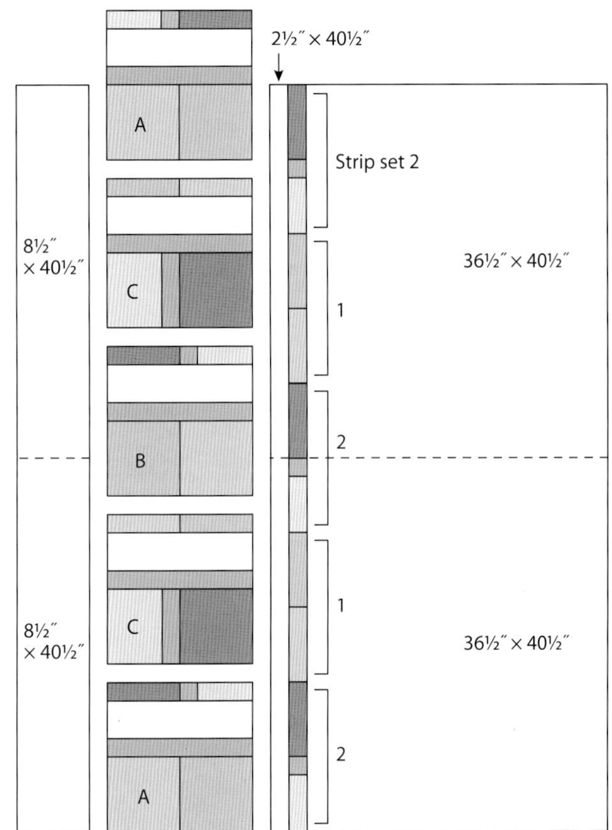

Quilt assembly

ÉCLAIRS

Éclairs uses 8″ Crispy Wonton blocks in a child-size grid setting. Blocks form links on a chain running horizontally across the quilt. Your eye may perceive the negative (background) spaces as the positive, revealing a secondary design of oblong éclair shapes.

Our fabric selection for *Éclairs* started with a large bundle of fat quarters representing the entire Mr. Roboto collection by Studio E Fabrics. The complementary color scheme of aqua and orange is grounded by dark gray and black. A light gray background contrasts well with all twelve print fabrics. We kept the color families together in groups of four blocks to keep the quilt from getting too visually wild. Since the aqua blocks demand the most attention, we lined them up in the center. Alternating the black and orange blocks asymmetrically provides balance. No fat quarter went unused! The extras appear on the back of *Éclairs* (page 124).

Éclairs is quilted in a cheerful overall design suitable for a child's quilt. Medium-value aqua thread that is neither too dark for the light background nor too light for the darker focus fabrics adds texture.

The warm orange binding lightens and brightens this happy quilt.

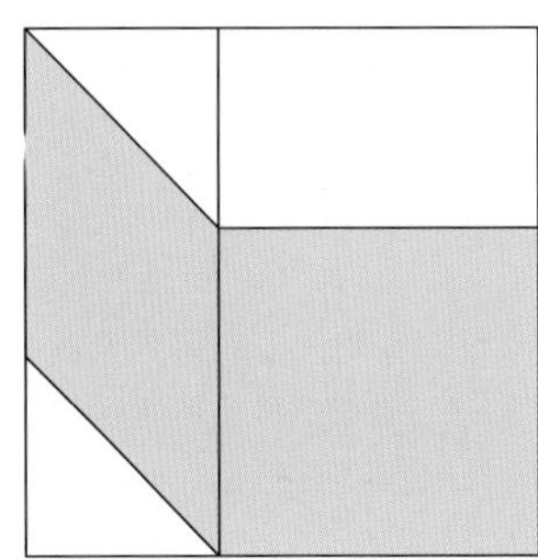

CRISPY WONTON BLOCK + GRID SETTING

Finished quilt:	**Finished block:**	**Number of blocks:**
48½″ × 64½″	8″ × 8″	48

Ingredients

These yardages are based on 42″ of usable width from nondirectional fabrics.

- **12 colors:** ⅓ yard each *or* 4 different fat quarters in each of 3 colors
- **Background:** 2⅛ yards if you use ⅓-yard color cuts *or* 1¾ yards if you use fat quarters as colors
- **Binding:** ½ yard (We used a warm orange.)
- **Quilt backing:** 57″ × 73″
- **Batting:** 57″ × 73″

Block Construction with Fat Quarters

If you use fat quarters, the strip sets will not be long enough to yield 4 segments. Cut 3 from each instead, and piece the fourth with the extra squares and rectangles listed in the cutting instructions.

Prep the Ingredients

Cut all fabrics by the width of fabric. Remove selvages before cutting.

FROM EACH COLOR:

If you use ⅓-yard pieces, from each:

- Cut 1 strip 5½″ × width of fabric.
- Cut 1 strip 3½″ × width of fabric.

  Subcut 4 rectangles 3½″ × 8½″.

If you use fat quarters, from each:

- Cut 1 strip 5½″ × 20″ for shortened strip set.
- Cut 1 strip 8½″ × 20″.

  Subcut 4 rectangles 8½″ × 3½″.

  Subcut 1 square 5½″ × 5½″ for fourth segment.

FROM BACKGROUND:

If you used ⅓-yard pieces for the color fabric:

- Cut 20 strips 3½″ × width of fabric.

  Set 12 strips aside for strip sets.

  From 8 strips, subcut 96 squares 3½″ × 3½″.

If you used fat quarters for the color fabric:

- Cut 16 strips 3½″ × width of fabric.

  Subcut 6 strips at the fold for shortened strip sets.

  From 2 strips, subcut 12 rectangles 3½″ × 5½″ for fourth segments.

  From 8 strips, subcut 96 squares 3½″ × 3½″.

FOR BINDING:

- Cut 6 strips 2½″ × width of fabric.

MAKE THE QUILT

Refer to Crispy Wonton Block Recipe (page 25) for the instructions to make 8˝ blocks.

1. From each color fabric, make 2 of Block A and 2 of Block B.

2. Referring to the quilt assembly diagram (below), arrange as desired.

3. Piece the blocks into 6 columns of 8 blocks each.

4. Sew the columns together to complete the quilt top.

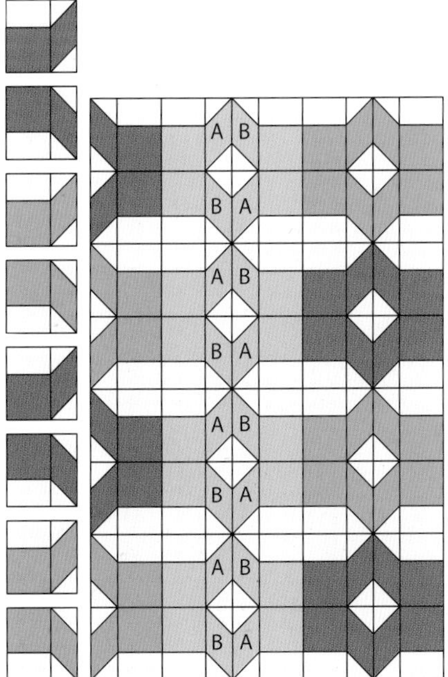

Quilt assembly

Éclairs, 48½˝ × 64½˝, made by Marny Buck, machine quilted by April West using the Around the Block pantograph by Kim Darwin, 2014

GLYCEMIC INDEX

Glycemic Index combines 16″ and 8″ Celery Sticks blocks. The blocks are staggered, placed directly next to one another with no additional sashing. These large-scale blocks create an exaggerated stair-step pyramid, while the smaller-scale blocks add a detail of depth. Think of it as a sugar high.

Balancing a few select multicolor values is sometimes challenging. We purposely placed the small-scale black print in the middle of the block, allowing the colors to rise and fall in a predictable rhythm. Architextures by Carolyn Friedlander for Robert Kaufman shares a common undertone but adds a pop of interest with a more saturated light green color. Warm colors next to cool colors create a vibrant juxtaposition.

The large-scale quilting pattern is a combination of curves and angles. It softens the sharp diagonals and fills the large negative space with subtle pattern and raised texture.

Scrappy binding gives the outer edge a connection to the central design. *Glycemic Index* is not to be taken so seriously; it's more casual and fun. Because the queen-sized quilt is square, you can turn the design in any direction to please your taste.

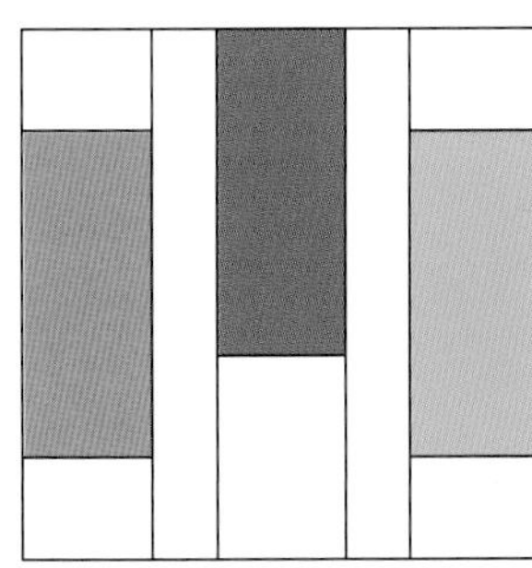

CELERY STICKS BLOCK + STAGGERED SETTING

Finished quilt:	**Finished blocks:**	**Number of blocks:**
96½″ × 96½″	8″ × 8″ and 16″ × 16″	4 blocks 8″ × 8″ and 6 blocks 16″ × 16″

Ingredients

These yardages are based on 42″ of usable width from nondirectional fabrics.

- **4 colors:** ¼ yard each (We used orange, fuchsia, medium green, and lime.)
- **Black:** ½ yard
- **Background:** 1⅓ yards for blocks and 6 yards for quilt setting pieces
- **Binding:** ¼ yard each of 4 colors *or* ⅞ yard of the same fabric
- **Quilt backing:** 105″ × 105″
- **Batting:** 105″ × 105″

Prep the Ingredients

Cut all fabrics by the width of fabric. Remove selvages before cutting.

FROM EACH COLOR:

- Cut 1 strip 4½″ × width of fabric.

  Subcut 3 rectangles 4½″ × 10½″ (16″ blocks).
- Cut 1 strip 2½″ × width of fabric.

  Subcut 2 rectangles 2½″ × 5½″ (8″ blocks).

FROM BLACK:

- Cut 2 strips 4½″ × width of fabric.

  Subcut 6 rectangles 4½″ × 10½″ (16″ blocks).
- Cut 1 strip 2½″ × width of fabric.

  Subcut 4 rectangles 2½″ × 5½″ (8″ blocks).

FROM BACKGROUND:

For blocks:

- Cut 2 strips 1½″ × width of fabric.

  Subcut 8 rectangles 1½″ × 8½″ (8″ blocks).
- Cut 8 strips 2½″ × width of fabric.

  From 1 strip, subcut 7 rectangles 2½″ × 3½″ (8″ blocks).

  From 1 strip, subcut 10 rectangles 2½″ × 2″ (8″ blocks).

  From 6 strips, subcut 12 rectangles 2½″ × 16½″ (16″ blocks).
- Cut 4 strips 4½″ × width of fabric.

  From 2 strips, subcut 18 rectangles 4½″ × 3½″ (16″ blocks).

  From 2 strips, subcut 9 rectangles 4½″ × 6½″ (16″ blocks).

For quilt setting pieces:

- Cut 12 strips 16½″ × width of fabric.

  From 4 strips, subcut 4 rectangles 16½″ × 40½″.

  From 1 strip, subcut 1 rectangle 16½″ × 36½″.

  From 1 strip, subcut 1 rectangle 16½″ × 24½″ and 2 rectangles 16½″ × 8½″.

  From 1 strip, subcut 1 rectangle 16½″ × 24½″ and 2 rectangles 8½″ × 4½″.

  From 3 strips, subcut 3 rectangles 16½″ × 32½″ and 2 squares 8½″ × 8½″.

  Using 2 strips and remaining partial strips from previous cuts, piece and subcut 2 rectangles 16½″ × 48½″.

FOR BINDING:

- Cut 10 strips 2½″ × width of fabric.

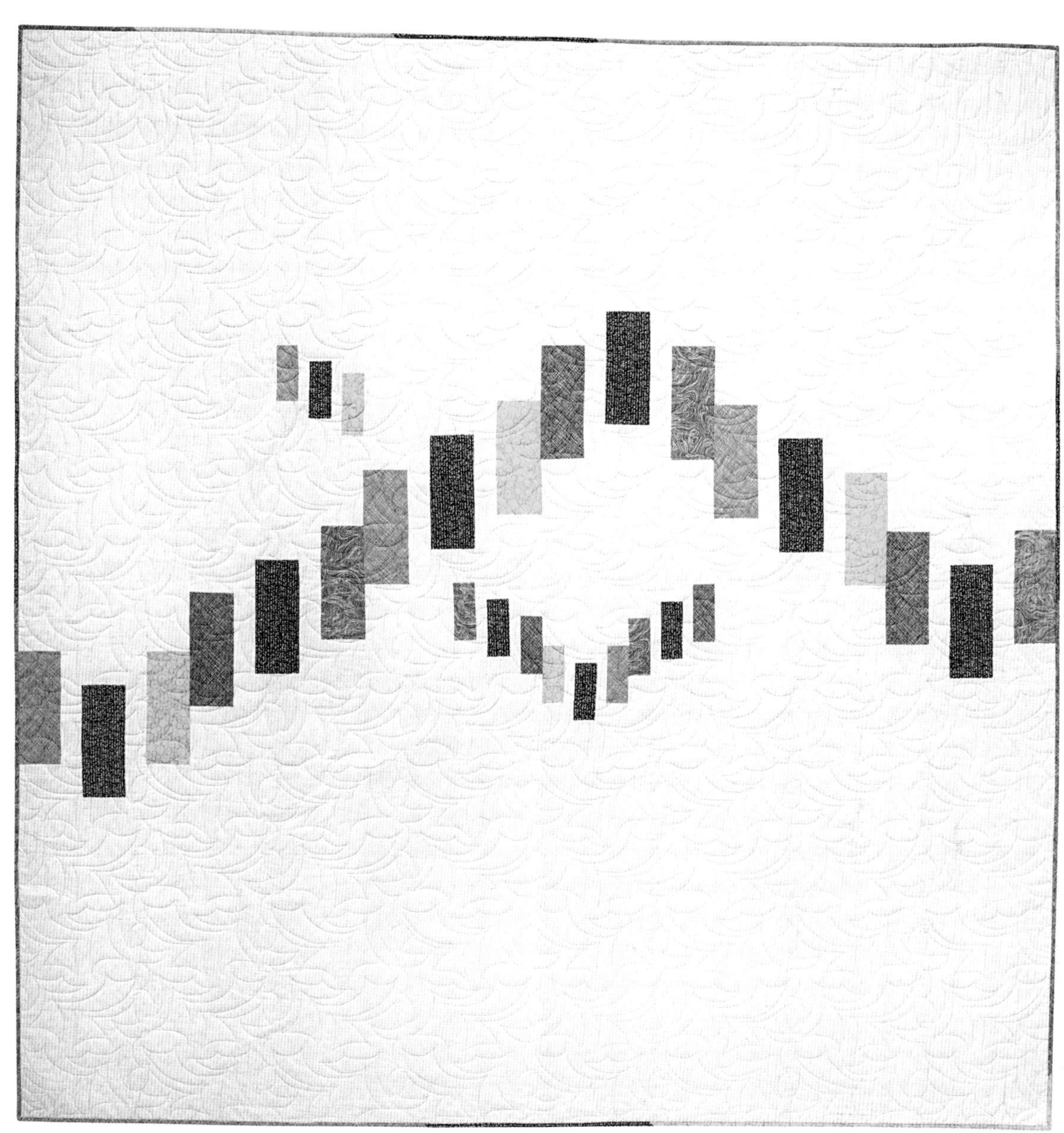

Glycemic Index, 96½″ × 96½″, made by Jill Guffy, machine quilted by April West using the Restless pantograph by Apricot Moon, 2014

Detail of *Glycemic Index*
(See project photo, page 109.)

MAKE THE QUILT

Since Glycemic Index *features a variety of fabrics, the Celery Sticks blocks for this quilt should be pieced individually. Refer to the Celery Sticks Block Recipe (page 28) for an explanation of A, B, and C blocks.*

1. Refer to the quilt assembly diagram to arrange the color rectangles, trying to balance color distribution and orientation. Depending on their positions in the blocks, sew either 1 larger or 2 smaller background rectangles to the color rectangles.

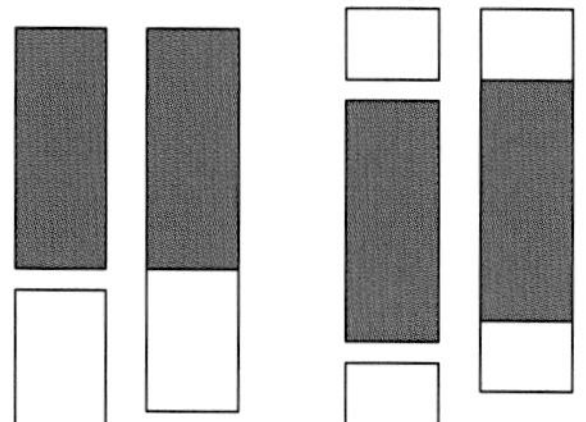

Detail of *Glycemic Index* (see project photo, page 109). Use multiple fabrics to make a lively binding.

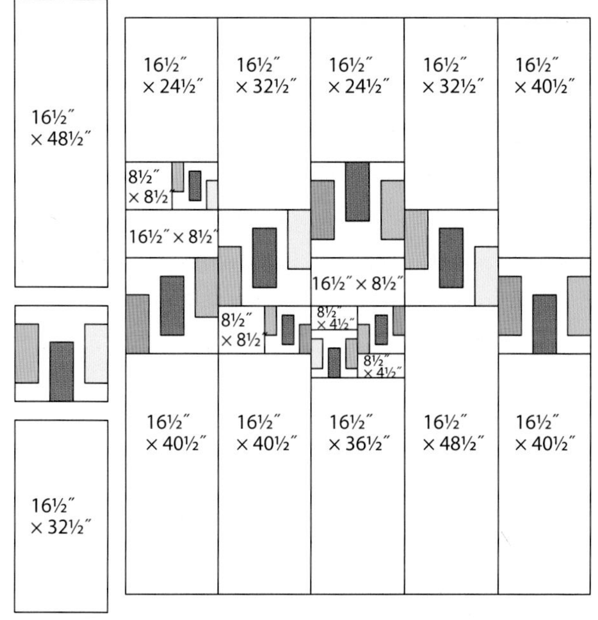

Quilt assembly

2. Sew the block background pieces (1½″ × 8½″, 2½″ × 16½″) between these pieced units to complete the blocks. For the 16″ blocks, make 2 A, 3 B, and 1 C. For the 8″ blocks, make 1 A, 1 B, and 2 C.

3. Arrange the blocks and remaining background pieces.

4. Piece the blocks and background pieces into columns.

5. Piece the columns together to complete the quilt top.

PETITS FOURS

*P*etits Fours is a sweet rendition of the It's a Wrap block. Four different fabrics form the outer edges of the block. The block's center fabric remains the same, contributing to the illusion of a line appearing to weave through the block. The accent line contrasts with the block, emphasizing this horizontal setting. Low-volume and small-scale block fabrics, all from Special Delivery by Studio 8 for Quilting Treasures, mix together for a blended recipe.

The playful yet organized finger shapes in the quilting appear organic. The thread color blends with the background for a subtle pattern and texture.

The accent color is repeated in the binding, reinforcing the strong horizontal lines of the interior.

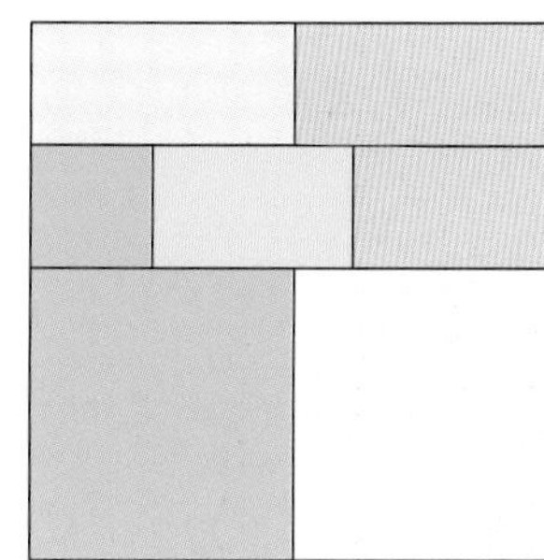

IT'S A WRAP BLOCK + REPEATED HORIZONTAL SETTING

Finished quilt:	Finished block:	Number of blocks:
40½″ × 52½″	8″ × 8″	8

Ingredients

These yardages are based on 42″ of usable width of fabric.

- **8 prints:** 9½″ × 9½″ square of each, with enough contrast in pattern and scale to allow edges to show when pieced
- **Background:** 1½ yards
- **Accent line:** ⅜ yard
- **Binding:** ½ yard (We used the accent fabric.)
- **Quilt backing:** 49″ × 61″
- **Batting:** 49″ × 61″

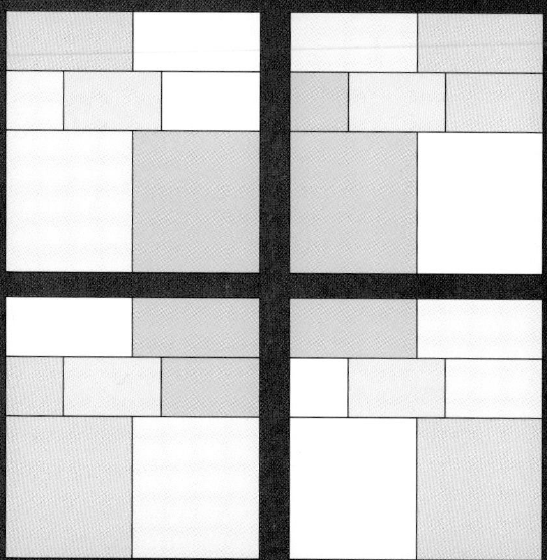

4 color arrangements, all with the same central rectangle

Prep the Ingredients

Cut all fabrics by the width of fabric unless otherwise stated. Remove selvages before cutting.

FROM PRINTS:

- Refer to Prep the Ingredients for 8″ Blocks (page 34) in It's a Wrap Block Recipe.

  Arrange 2 stacks of 4 fabrics each, making sure there is contrast in pattern and scale between adjacent fabrics. Follow the stack-cutting directions for the 8″ It's a Wrap block, cutting 4 fabrics at a time instead of 5. Repeat for the second stack of 4 fabrics. Keep the cut fabrics in their respective stacks. See Make the Block (page 36) for instructions on shuffling the fabrics.

FROM BACKGROUND FABRIC:

- Cut 3 strips 2½″ × width of fabric.
- Cut 8 strips 4½″ × width of fabric.

  Set aside 3 strips for strip sets.

  Subcut 5 strips 4½″ × 40½″.

FROM ACCENT LINE:

- Cut 4 strips 2½″ × width of fabric.

  Set aside 3 strips for strip sets.

  From 1 strip, subcut 8 rectangles 3½″ × 2½″.

FOR BINDING:

- Cut 5 strips 2½″ × width of fabric.

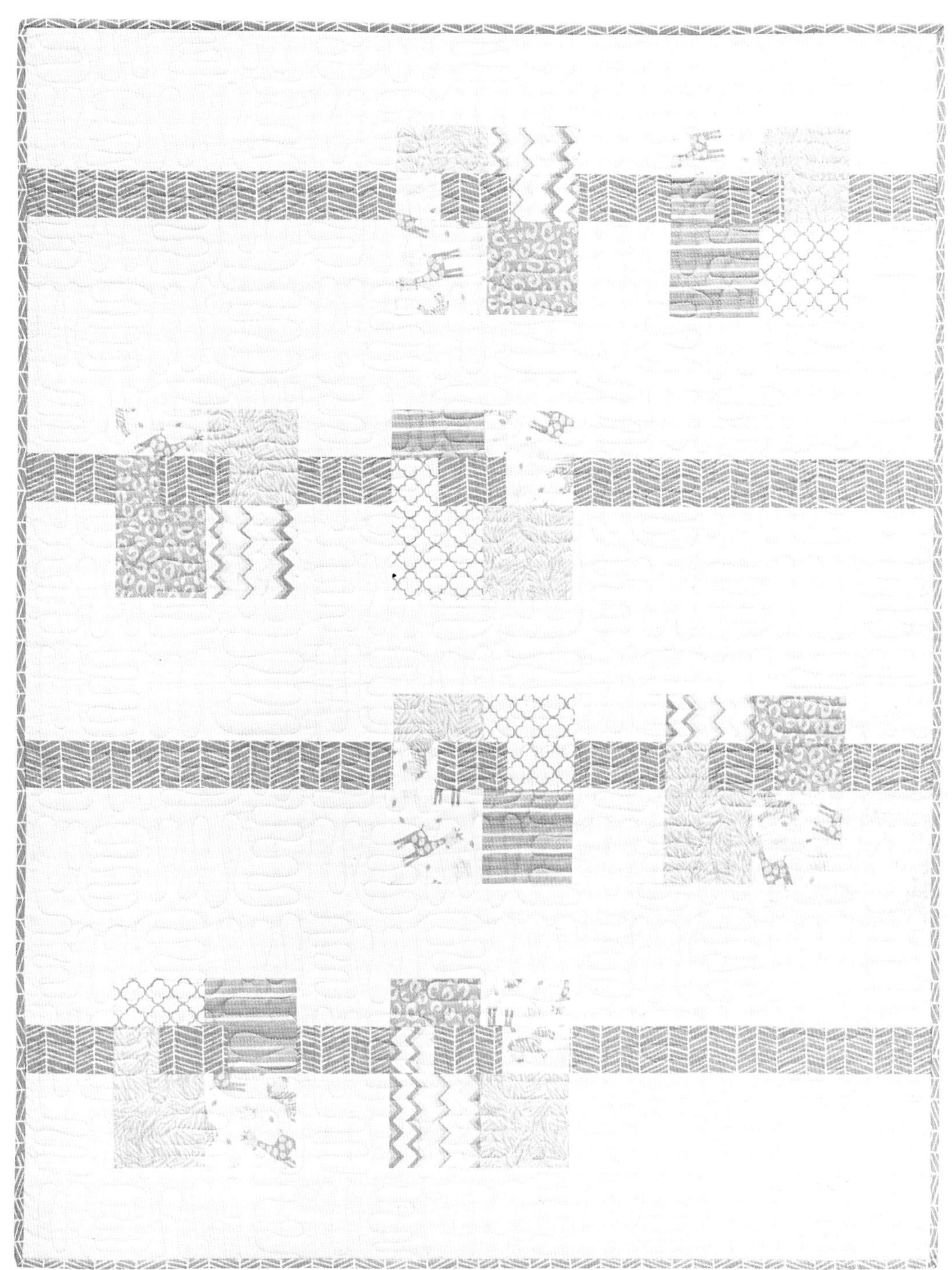

Petits Fours, 40½″ × 56½″, made by Jill Guffy, machine quilted by April West using the Ribbon Candy pantograph by Linda's Electric Quilters, 2014

MAKE THE QUILT

Refer to It's a Wrap Block Recipe, Make the Block (page 36), for the instructions for making 8″ blocks.

1. From each stack, remove the block's center rectangles and replace them with a 4-stack of 3½″ × 2½″ rectangles from the accent line fabric.

2. In each stack, shuffle the outside pieces as described in It's a Wrap Block Recipe, Step 1 (page 36). All 4 prints plus the accent should be visible on the top of each stack.

3. Move the stacks next to the sewing machine.

4. Piece 8 blocks, taking care to keep the rows in the order in which they are stacked.

5. Sew the rows together to complete 8 blocks.

6. Sew a 2½″ accent strip between a 2½″ background strip and a 4½″ background strip. Make 3 strip sets.

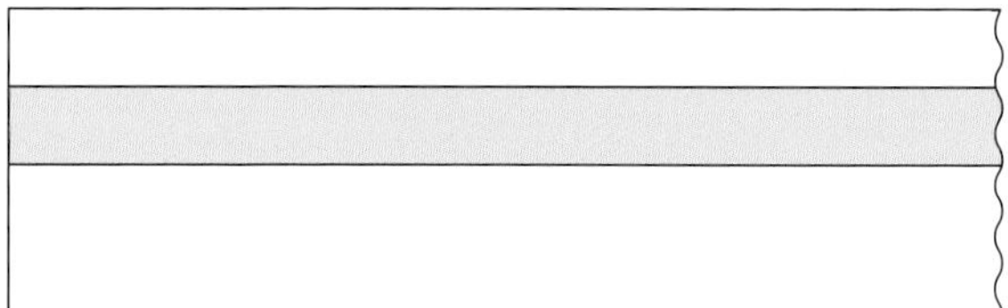

7. From the 3 strip sets, cut 4 segments at 16½″ intervals and 8 segments at 4½″ intervals.

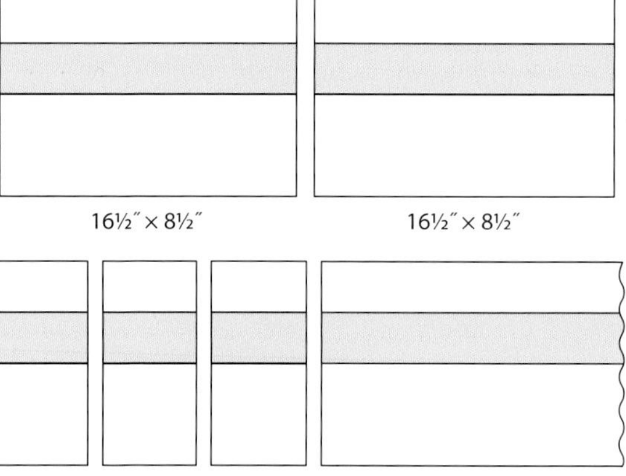

Detail of *Petits Fours* (See project photo, page 115.)

8. Referring to the quilt assembly diagram, arrange the blocks, strip-set segments, and background setting pieces. Position the blocks so that the accent line appears to run straight through both the strip-set segments and the blocks.

9. Sew the strip sets and blocks into rows.

10. Sew the pieced rows together with the background rows to complete the quilt top.

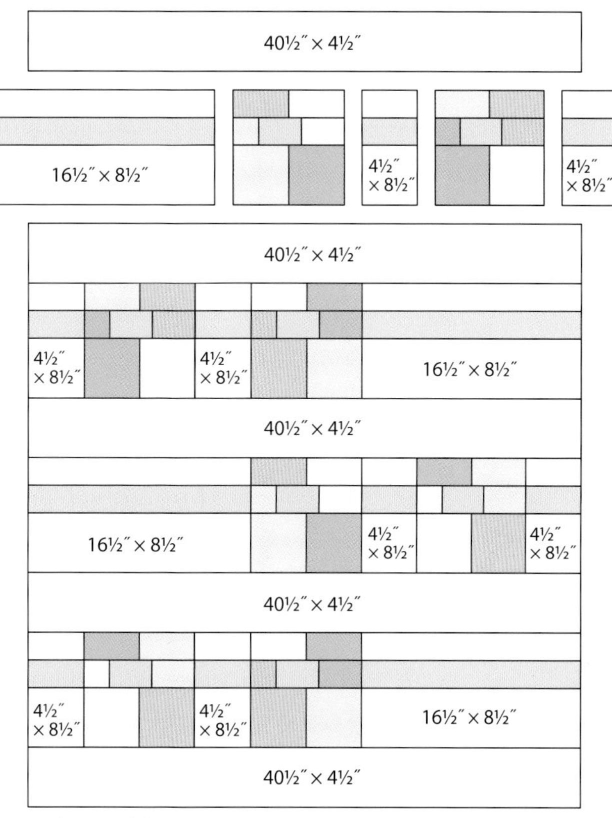

Quilt assembly

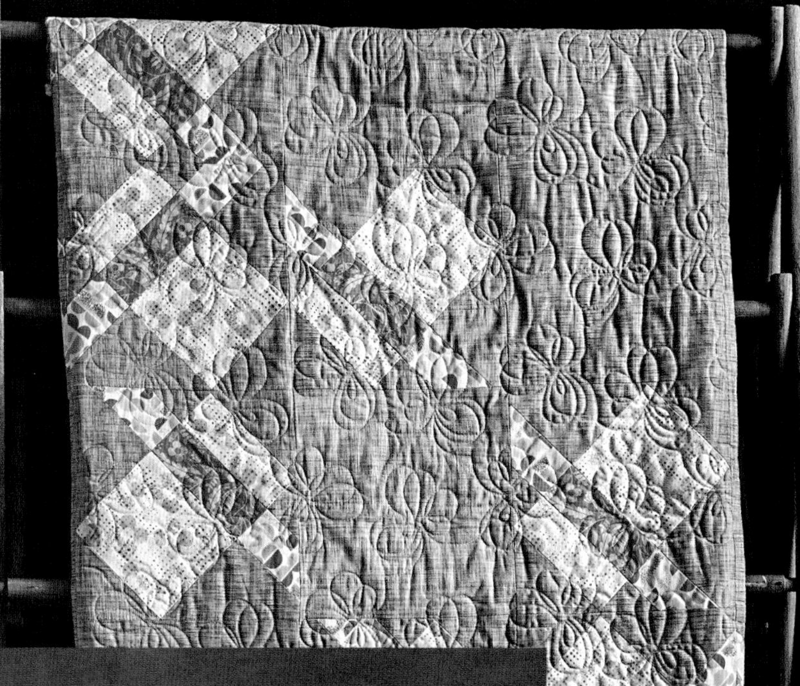

SWEET ENDINGS

Sweet Endings features 12 Sushi blocks in the baby-sized diagonal setting. The result is a diagonally symmetrical quilt, with a pleasing asymmetry remaining within each block. One position in the diagonal setting diagram (page 77) is filled with a background square rather than a pieced block. Using the contrasting background square in this position causes a secondary shape to form in the center of the quilt; the negative becomes a subtle positive.

We chose fresh, fun fabrics in light, medium, and dark from the Palermo collection by Erin McMorris for Free Spirit. The textured gray background contrasts well with the three block fabrics.

Light pink quilting lines create a lively floral pattern across the surface of the quilt. The scale of the flowers suits the scale of the block and provides an overall texture.

The medium-value, multicolor fabric in the binding brightens both the edge of the quilt and the large areas of negative space.

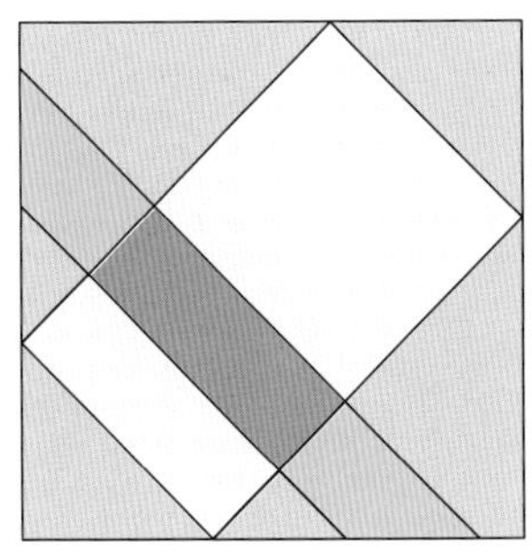

SUSHI BLOCK + DIAGONAL SETTING

Finished quilt:	Finished block:	Number of blocks:
40½″ × 40½″	8″ × 8″	12

Ingredients

- **Light (white print):** ½ yard
- **Medium (multi print):** ½ yard
- **Dark (pink):** ¼ yard if nondirectional, ½ yard if directional
- **Background (gray):** ¾ yard for blocks and ⅞ yard for quilt setting pieces
- **Binding:** ½ yard (We used the multi print.)
- **Quilt backing:** 49″ × 49″
- **Batting:** 49″ × 49″

These yardages are based on 42″ of usable width of fabric, with nondirectional fabric for the background. You can use directional fabrics for the light, medium, and dark fabrics. See Using Stripes (page 41).

Prep the Ingredients

Cut all fabrics by the width of fabric unless otherwise stated. Remove selvages before cutting.

FROM LIGHT:

- Cut 2 strips 6½″ × width of fabric.

  Subcut 12 rectangles 6½″ × 4¾″.

FROM MEDIUM:

- Cut 4 strips 5″ × *length* of fabric to yield 4 rectangles 5″ × 18″.

FROM DARK:

- If nondirectional, cut 1 strip 4¾″ × width of fabric.

  Subcut 2 rectangles 4¾″ × 21″.

- If directional, cut 2 strips 4¾″ × *length* of fabric to yield 2 rectangles 4¾″ × 18″.

FOR BINDING:

- Cut 5 strips 2½″ × width of fabric.

FROM BACKGROUND:

For blocks:

- Cut 2 strips 7″ × width of fabric.

  Subcut 12 squares 7″ × 7″.

  Subcut each square once diagonally to yield 24 large triangles.

- Cut 2 strips 5″ × width of fabric.

  Subcut 12 squares 5″ × 5″.

  Subcut each square once diagonally to yield 24 small triangles.

For quilt setting pieces:

- Cut 3 strips 8½″ × width of fabric.

  From 2 strips, subcut 2 rectangles 8½″ × 24½″ and 2 rectangles 8½″ × 16½″.

  From 1 strip, subcut 3 squares 8½″ × 8½″.

MAKE THE QUILT

Refer to Sushi Block Recipe, Make the Block (page 41), for the instructions for making 8″ blocks.

1. Make 12 Sushi blocks.

2. Referring to the quilt assembly diagram, arrange blocks with background pieces.

3. Sew the blocks and background pieces into columns.

4. Sew the columns together to complete the quilt top.

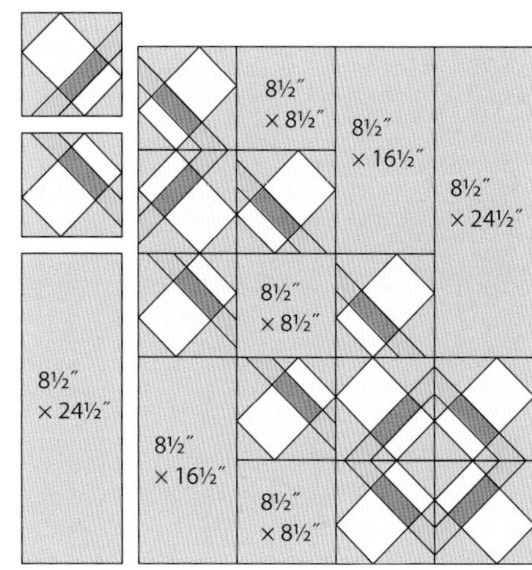

Quilt assembly

Sweet Endings, 40½″ × 40½″, made by Marny Buck, machine quilted by April West using the Petalism pantograph by Jodi Beamish, 2014

SAVORY

BACKING SUGGESTIONS

Who doesn't flip to the back of a quilt to see what surprises take shape? Is it an extension of the front or a completely different flavor?

The names of the backs are reminiscent of family meals served on those regular weeknight venues. *Leftovers* comes to mind, but we've already used that in one of our successful patterns! *Goulash* was never really a recipe—just a loosely used term for a hamburger hot dish. You get the idea.

In constructing our backs, we follow several formulas that help us create something beyond the usual single fabric back:

- For the most part, **we quilt by checkbook.** The quilt tops are out of our hands for a short visit to another cook, a wonderful long-arm quilter. Her flavors, with our input, enhance the recipe. To determine our quilt backing size, we always add 8″ vertically and 8″ horizontally (4″ for each side) to the size of the quilt top.
- Often, **we add a column or row** to a width of fabric to bring it up to size. We split the width of fabric asymmetrically so that the row or column does not end up centered. It is either to the left or right side or the upper or lower third of the quilt.
- **Leave the selvages to the outside** when splitting a width of fabric. This gives the quilter a nice handle without fraying fabric, and you can trim them later.
- **When using scraps, lay them out on a large surface** to help define the direction or plan. Arrange and rearrange, add and discard until you get a desired outcome. Don't get too picky. This is somewhat improvisational; part of the fun is the unexpected!

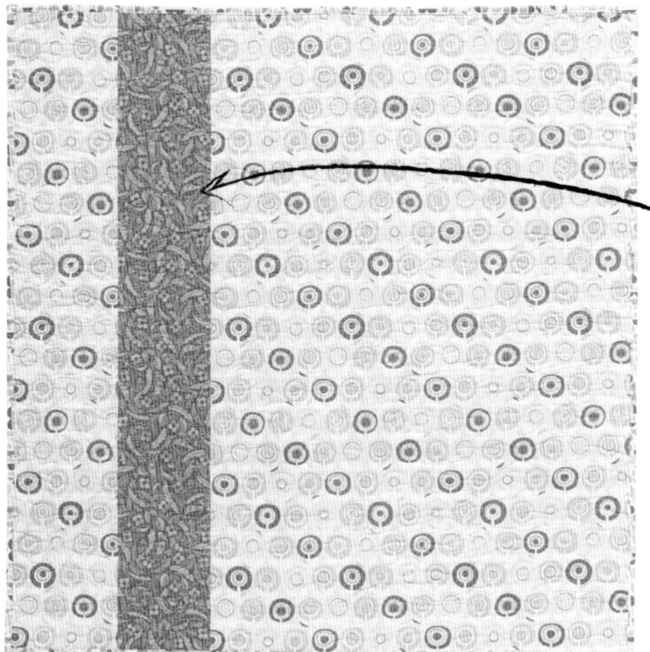

Stretching the Dollar, the back of *Sweet Endings*
(See project photo, page 121.)

The quick fix seen in Budget Meal and Stretching the Dollar is a single line of fabric added to increase either the length or the width of the back. Often this simple solution is enough to bring the backing up to size. It's just a dab of modern.

Budget Meal, the back of *Tempting Turnovers*
(See project photo, page 93.)

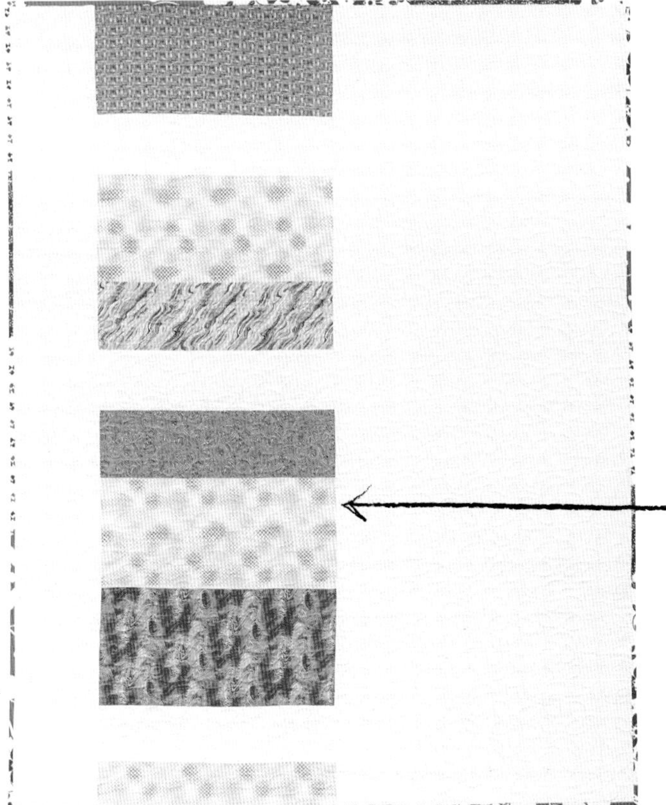

Remnants from our stash reinforce the *Easy as Pie* color scheme. A single wide column of assorted rectangles adds interest and size to Raiding the Pantry.

Raiding the Pantry, the back of *Easy as Pie* (See project photo, page 99.)

Three large-scale *Dippers* arrangements are combined in a horizontal row. The cook didn't give the quilter the final recipe to center the backing, so it ended up Over the Edge. Communication is the key!

Six fat quarters remained in the bundle used for *Éclairs*. Not wanting any to go to waste, we squared and bordered each on two sides with solids, and placed them in alternating positions in Clean Your Plate.

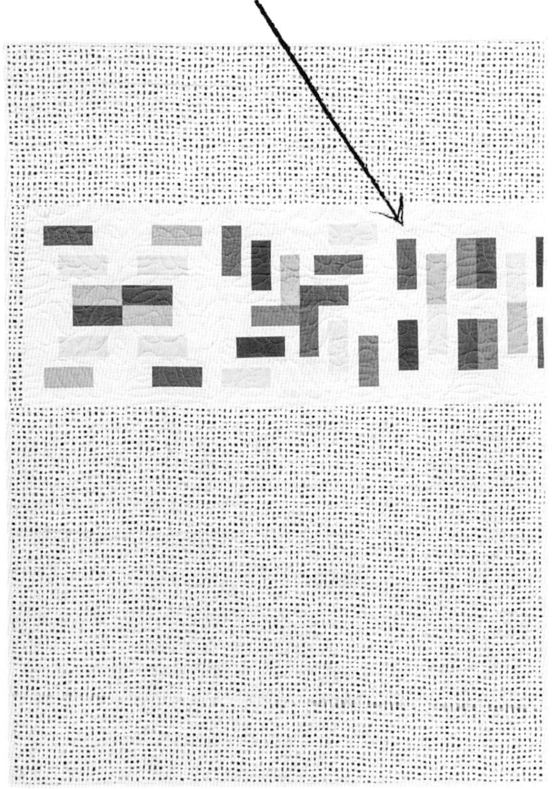

Over the Edge, the back of *Dippers* (See project photo, page 59.)

Clean Your Plate, the back of *Éclairs* (See project photo, page 105.)

Experimental *Bottle Stoppers* blocks follow a different recipe in Rehash. Vertically stacked, they are surrounded with a contrasting value of orange and a vibrant floral from Nomad by Jen Fox for P&B Textiles. The asymmetry on either side of the column of blocks is intentional and pronounced.

Rehash, the back of *Bottle Stoppers* (See project photo, page 55.)

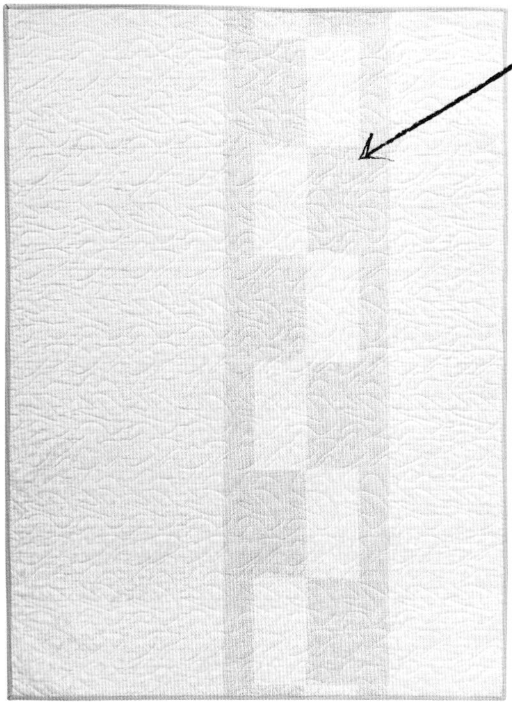

A simple strip set of background and a coordinating fabric is sliced, alternated, and served up on Set the Table. The width of the column brings a single length of fabric up to size.

Set the Table, the back of *Spring Rolls*
(See project photo, page 67.)

Supersize It, the back of *Snack Circuit* (See project photo, page 51.)

Supersize It replicates a large-scale Salsa block.

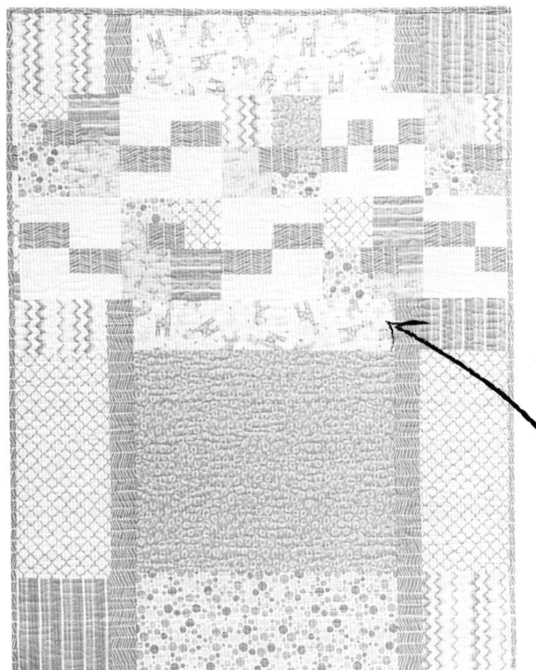

Goulash, the back of *Petits Fours*
(See project photo, page 115.)

Goulash is one of those recipes where you just keep adding and tasting and hoping for the best. Take it or leave it.

Background fabric and quarter-square triangles from 10″ squares of Daily Zen by Michele D'Amore for Benartex are sewn to triangles of black from the same collection. The resulting chevron will Sharpen Your Appetite. Presented asymmetrically, the additional black line balances the design.

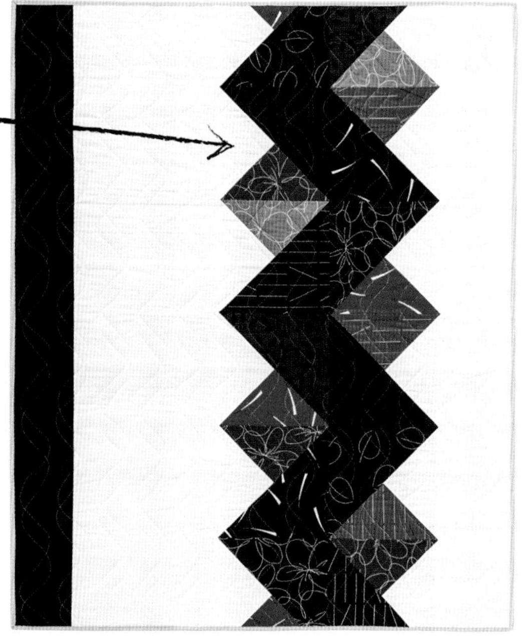

Sharpen Your Appetite, the back of *Antipasto*
(See project photo, page 47.)

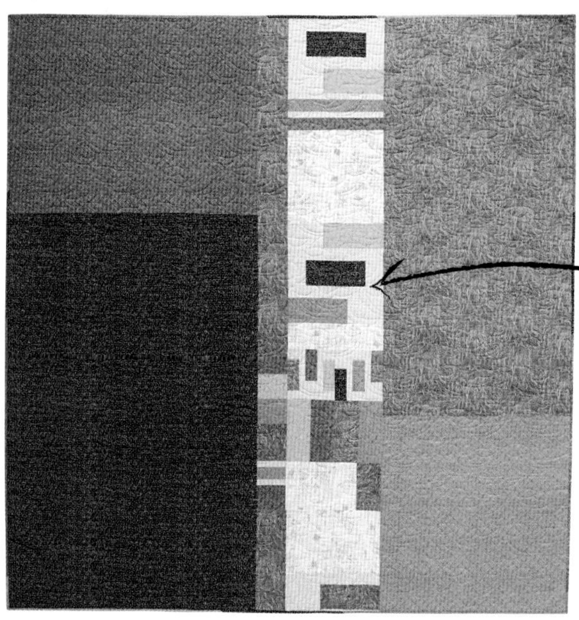

Lunch Counter, the back of *Glycemic Index*
(See project photo, page 109.)

Glycemic Index practice blocks are on today's menu. Line them all up, and then use the width-of-fabric cuts to balance. Cold sandwiches are opposite the hot entrées at the Lunch Counter.

You've seen it once, now you are going to get it again. Adding other fresh fabrics from the Color Composition collection by Studio RK for Robert Kaufman Fabrics reinforces the original *Mondrian Morsels* recipe here in Encore Serving.

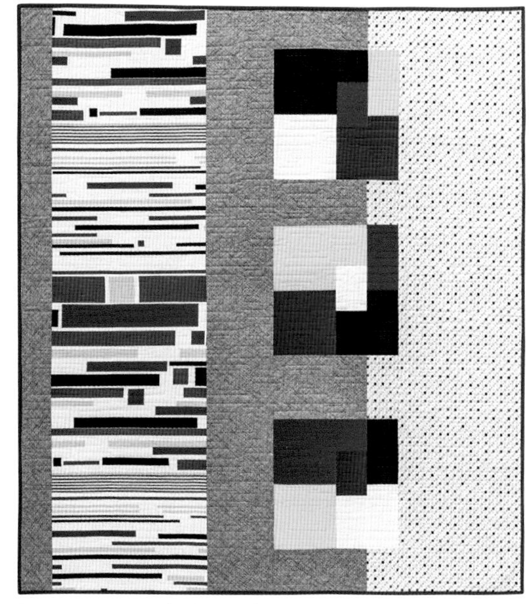

Encore Serving, the back of *Mondrian Morsels*
(See project photo, page 63.)

ABOUT *the* AUTHORS

More than six years ago, Marny Buck and Jill Guffy created Modern Quilt Relish. Inspired by simple shapes and colors, food, and sewing, they have designed a line of more than 20 patterns and actively publish, blog, and teach about quilting. Working together offers two sets of eyes and tag-team assignments. Marny enjoys the challenge of technology, and for that, Jill is willing to pay the bills. They live in Ames, Iowa, with their husbands and love spending time with family and their adorable grandchildren.

Visit Marny and Jill at

MODERNQUILTRELISH.BLOGSPOT.COM

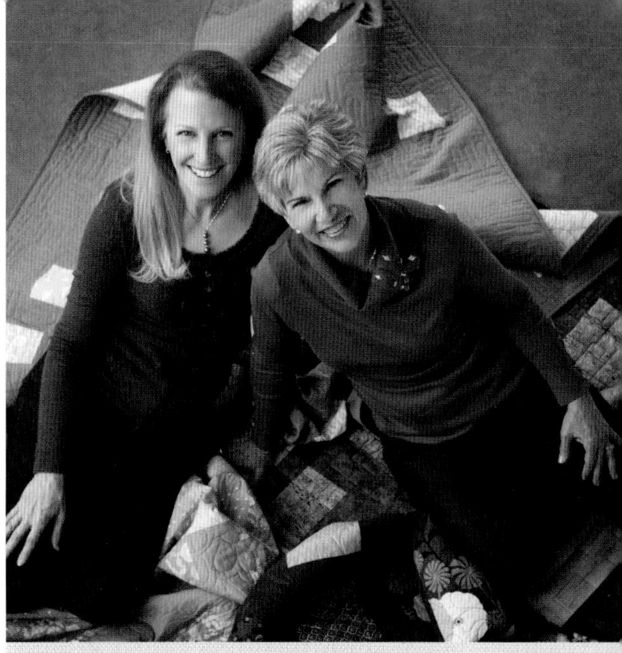

MARNY BUCK AND JILL GUFFY

Photo by Jacquelyn Olson, Jacquelyn's Photography, Ames, Iowa

RESOURCES

The first place to go for information and products is your local quilt shop. If that is not possible or they cannot help you, then try the Internet for information.

READING FOR BEGINNING QUILTERS

From C&T Publishing:

Books:

The Practical Guide to Patchwork by Elizabeth Hartman
Start Quilting with Alex Anderson

Web resources:

ctpub.com/quilting-sewing-tips >
Downloads: "How to Finish Your Quilt"

MACHINE-QUILTING PANTOGRAPHS

Apricot Moon
apricotmoon.com

Hermione Agee
Jodi Beamish
Kristin Hoftyzer
Norma Woods Sharp
quiltscomplete.com

Kim Darwin
longarmuniversity.com

Linda's Electric Quilters
longarmsupplies.net

Timeless Quilting Designs
timelessquiltingdesigns.com.au

Urban Elementz
urbanelementz.com

FABRICS

Benartex
benartex.com

Dear Stella Design
dearstelladesign.com

FreeSpirit Fabrics
freespiritfabric.com

In the Beginning Fabrics
inthebeginningfabrics.com

P&B Textiles
pbtex.com.com

Robert Kaufman Fabrics
robertkaufman.com

Studio E Fabrics
studioefabrics.com

Quilting Treasures
quiltingtreasures.com

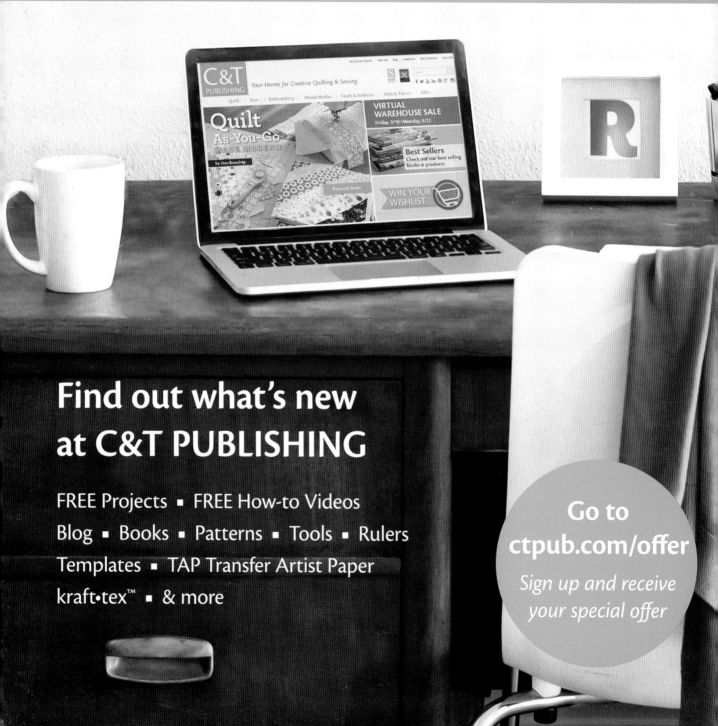